DREAM IT
DARE IT
DO IT

HEARSTBOOKS

An Imprint of Sterling Publishing
1166 Avenue of the Americas
New York, NY 10036

COSMOPOLITAN is a registered trademark of Hearst Communications, Inc.

Text © 2016 by Hearst Communications, Inc.

ISBN 978-1-61837-204-8

Distributed in Canada by Sterling Publishing
c/o Canadian Manda Group, 664 Annette Street
Toronto, Ontario, Canada M6S 2C8
Distributed in the United Kingdom by GMC Distribution Services
Castle Place, 166 High Street, Lewes, East Sussex, England BN7 1XU
Distributed in Australia by Capricorn Link (Australia) Pty. Ltd.
P.O. Box 704, Windsor, NSW 2756, Australia

For information about custom editions, special sales, and premium and
corporate purchases, please contact Sterling Special Sales at 800-805-5489
or specialsales@sterlingpublishing.com.

Manufactured in China

2 4 6 8 10 9 7 5 3 1

www.sterlingpublishing.com

DREAM IT
DARE IT
DO IT

CONTENTS

fun fearless life

Start off with this inspiring pep talk from Cosmo's Editor-in-Chief.

WHAT YOU'RE HOLDING IN YOUR HANDS ISN'T JUST A BOOK— it's a guide to your life.

Every month, Cosmo packs smart, actionable advice into our pages, and with this collection of our most practical, doable tips, you get a road map to the life you want—your Fun, Fearless Life.

All through this special edition, brilliant experts from all walks of life share their tricks for shaking things up and taking the first steps toward making your dreams a reality. Running your Fun Fearless Life is a bit like running the business of you...and for that you need money!

So check out our career advice for how to get ahead doing work you love...and get paid well for it. That way, at the end of your workweek, you can let loose with your friends, your love, or whoever else you want.

Living a Fun, Fearless Life also means knowing how to decorate your place (p. 170), getting a few delicious (and impressive) recipes in your arsenal (p. 194), and learning the secrets to throwing an unforgettable party (p. 212). Plus, it's about expanding your perspective by seeing other parts of the world, so we've also got the scoop on everything you need to know to plan an adventure— whether it's a road trip or flying to a far-flung destination.

So get ready to kick things up a notch, starting now.

Joanna Coles
EDITOR-IN-CHIEF

1

1
DREAM IT,
THEN DO IT

Fun
Fearless
Life:
A USER'S GUIDE

STEP 1

**Get inspired by
Mika Brzezinski.**

STEPS 2 TO 10

**Follow our smart, do-this-now,
five-step plans for everything
from finding love to unlocking
your inner CEO.**

STEP 11

Enjoy being a rock star.

— MIKA BRZEZINSKI, CO-HOST
OF MSNBC'S *MORNING JOE*

THE ONLY WAY to have the fun, fearless life you crave and deserve is by respecting yourself and your potential and making sure everyone else does. In my book, *Knowing Your Value*, I wrote about the ways that I, like many women, held myself back career-wise by undervaluing myself. Knowing your worth—and acting like it—is essential to success at work and happiness on a personal level. Here's how to lay the groundwork for your incredible career and love life.

KNOW YOUR VALUE 101

START STRONG.
Not having a ton of skill and experience doesn't mean you don't have inherent value, so act like you do. Make clear that you have gumption, an interest in learning, and a willingness to work hard.

MAKE THE BEST DAMN COFFEE.
Regardless of where you are in the pecking order, take responsibility for the tasks assigned to you and do them like a rock star. If you're getting someone coffee, get their order exactly right.

DON'T LET YOUR JOB BE A BAD BOYFRIEND.
Women, unlike men, don't always know when their value is rising and when it's time to push for more at work. Being overly helpful and eager, or waiting for

your boss to promote you, is like waiting for a bad boyfriend to propose. In both cases, if you allow people to step on you, they will.

WORK IT IN ROMANCE.
Make your voice heard in love too. If something in your relationship is subpar and you don't respect yourself enough to speak up, your partner will assume you don't expect better.

CHANGE IT.
Upgrade how people see you with a few simple physical cues. Don't hunch, speak clearly, look people directly in the eyes, and get your hair out of your face! Practice by doing dry runs of scary conversations in the mirror.

Break Bad Emotional Habits
(I.E., GET YOUR BITCH ON A LEASH)

1.
Eliminate the embarrassment you have about whatever you're trying to change. If it's secret and hidden, it's tougher to kick.

2.
Identify how the habit talks to you. Addicted to sweets? What does the cookie say to you to get into your mouth? Does it say, C'mon, you deserve this? Separating the impulse helps you more clearly identify it when it strikes. The next time you want a cookie, you'll hear that voice as temptation, not as a command from on high that you must obey.

— LAUREN ZANDER,
CHAIRMAN OF
THE HANDEL GROUP

3.
Nickname it,

4.
and put it in its place. If you know you can be a bitch, call that Ms. Bitch. This dismantles some of the habit's power and helps you stop defending the behavior. You go from saying, "I had to yell at my roommate. She drank my wine again and that's disrespectful" to "Ms. Bitch is trying to make trouble with my roomie. But I'm in control, not her." Isolating the habit helps you address the negative impulse when it arises.

5.
Create a consequence for acting out the habit. For example, promise to go an extra mile on the treadmill if Ms. Bitch shows up. That way, you've paid the piper and you're free to move forward and not feel guilty about it.

Unlock Your Inner CEO

GET YOUR "BOD" IN SHAPE

Create a personal board of directors—people you respect, with whom you can be authentic, and who can help you further your career. Cultivate these relationships, so your mentors become invested in seeing you thrive.

IMPRESS YOURSELF FIRST

Think about what will knock your socks off before you think about giving other people what you think they want from you. When we are working to make ourselves proud of our own efforts and for the joy of it, we break the mold and produce extraordinary results.

MAKE A TOP THREE LIST

Write down the three leaders you find most influential, then list the attributes that make each of them so powerful. Tack that list up in a place you see every day as a reminder to bring those attributes into your daily life.

SPEAK WITH PURPOSE

Take time to cook up what you are really thinking and want to communicate before you start filling conversational silences. You'll be received more powerfully and become a more confident speaker.

LOOK TO LEAD

Seek opportunities to lead people. Head a team on a small project or lead a volunteer group—anything that will give you some practice.

— MEREDITH HABERFELD, FOUNDER AND CEO OF MEREDITH HABERFELD COACHING; CAREER COACH TO EXECUTIVES OF JPMORGAN CHASE, CREDIT SUISSE, AND THE WORLD HEALTH ORGANIZATION

Tweet Smarter

Break through by being colorful and confident and sticking to what you know.

DO A DATE LIST. What makes you irresistible? Are you witty? Intellectual? Narrow a list to five qualities.

DO A JOB LIST. Are you the go-to gal for sex tips or sci-fi movies? List your top five areas of expertise.

LEARN THE DRILL. Get the hashtags, handles, and lingo for your job list so you can connect with like-minded people. Otherwise, you're just a voice in the wilderness, darling.

BUILD YOUR PROFILE. For one month, talk about the things on your job list, and show the qualities from your date list.

HAVE FUN WITH IT! Once you're tweeting confidently, people will be interested in what you have to say. Enjoy your millions of followers, lady!

— TOM FITZGERALD & LORENZO MARQUEZ,
TOMANDLORENZO.COM

Get Lucky

— JASON SILVA, HOST OF
BRAIN GAMES ON
NATIONAL GEOGRAPHIC

Think yourself lucky! Leverage your brain's pattern-recognition capacity to make your dreams come true. (Hang on. This will make sense in a sec.) Basically, tell your brain what to watch out for and you'll be more likely to notice those things when you come across them.

Think about what you want to achieve.

Write it down.

Add people, events, and things that could help you achieve your goal.

Prime your brain to be on the lookout by rereading your list every morning.

When "luck" strikes and something on your list crosses your path, act! Jump! Get it!

Make A Love Plan

▶ **Treat your romance like a friend and your friends like a romance.** Release pressure from a romantic relationship by acting like you would with a friend. You'll be more authentic and relaxed. And prioritizing friendships by making dates and putting in effort also takes pressure off the romance by making you less emotionally needy.

▶ **Leave a good-energy imprint.** Measure the success of your date by how much fun you have, not by how cool or hot you were. When you have a great time, the other person feels that, which creates a positive-energy imprint.

—GABRIELLE BERNSTEIN, *NEW YORK TIMES* BEST-SELLER, LIFE COACH, AND AUTHOR OF THE BOOK *MIRACLES NOW*

▶ **Have a sober date** (stick with us here): Physically active dates produce memories from the experience, which last longer and create a bond.

▶ **Forgive your past relationships.** If you're carrying resentment from your last relationship, it will get repurposed in your current one. Letting go of those past dramas allows you to get rid of your baggage. Forgive your exes to give your current or future boyfriend a chance.

What Should You Really Be?

—MEG JAY, PHD,
AUTHOR OF *THE DEFINING DECADE*

"Follow your dreams." Everyone says it's the key to happiness. But what if your dream is hazy? While you have more career options than previous generations, the possibilities can be vast to the point of being paralyzing. The key to navigating the angst is identity capital, which you're already earning just by living your life: doing a semester abroad, volunteering at the animal shelter....The challenge is to become more involved in things that you know interest you and to leverage all that to achieve your dreams. Here's my 3-step plan to get on the right path:

STEP 1. FIND WHAT'S REAL

GO BACK TO THE BEGINNING
Picture your former and future selves and find a common thread between them. Think about how you spent free time as a kid and classes you happily aced in college.

SURVEY YOUR SKILLS
Consider compliments you've received from teachers and bosses. This will help you zero in on goals to which you have an emotional connection. What would feel most exciting for you to talk about with friends?

STEP 2. LINE UP YOUR DUCKS

SET LIMITS
Make a list of three to five different plans based on the clues from your kid self and the future you. (Too few will feel limiting; too many, daunting.)

TAKE IT FOR A TEST DRIVE
So you've always loved kids and swimming? Consider getting certified to teach swimming lessons with the goal of starting your own after-school program. Or if you've always loved jewelry, apply to be an intern or assistant at a fashion house to learn how the industry really works.

STEP 3. MAKE IT HAPPEN

CONNECT
Reach out to the people you don't know that well. I call them your weak ties—acquaintances, friends of friends. New opportunities are more likely to come from these ties than from your besties.

SET A TIME LINE
Give yourself six months to a year to take action. When time's up, assess if this path is working. Deadlines and goals don't sound sexy, but they are our dreams in actionable steps. And acting on your dreams is definitely sexy!

Break Out of Your Comfort Zone

Sometimes, something scary stands between you and the thing you want. **Jillian Michaels** tells you how to push through it.

WHEN I STARTED PLANNING MY FIRST LIVE SHOW, *Maximize Your Life*, going onstage seemed terrifying. But I really wanted a direct connection where I could talk to people, look them in the eye, and hug them. So I studied, rehearsed, surrounded myself with a great tour team...and it was as terrifying as I'd feared! But it keeps getting better—now I'm hooked.

It's been another lesson that the amount of happiness and meaning in your life directly relates to how you manage fear and vulnerability. You can't get the promotion unless you ask for it. You can't have better sex until you are open with your partner. And it doesn't matter whether the hard thing you have to do is physical or emotional—hard is hard and fear is fear.

When I want to do something that scares me, I walk through these steps. Try it—then have that conversation, sign up for that coding class, start training for your first 5K. And then enjoy the sweet victory when your risk-taking work pays off.

> **"Treat yourself as you would someone you love."**
> —JILLIAN MICHAELS

FIGURE OUT YOUR WHY

When people say they want to be healthy "just because," that's a blanket answer with no real meaning, so it won't provide any real motivation. You have to define what healthy is to you. Is it looking hot in skinny jeans—getting noticed instead of feeling overlooked? Is it about avoiding health problems you've seen in your family? You'll never tolerate the how—the tough things you have to do to achieve your goal—without feeling a deep, emotional link to the why.

MANAGE THE FEAR

Psych yourself up for a challenge by thinking through the end game. Imagine three possible scenarios: (A) You do nothing, (B) you do it and it goes badly, or (C) you do it and have success. Play that out and you'll see that you have to go for it. Say it's time to have a talk with a new guy about making things more official. You're ready for the real deal but nervous! In scenario A, you chicken out. But keeping quiet makes you more resentful, resulting in your original fear—you break up. In scenario B, you talk and don't get the answer you want, but you can move on to new guys and possibilities. Last, C: You do it and you get the real, honest relationship you're looking for!

BE NICE

I used to give my 4-year-old daughter a time-out when she didn't listen. That worked okay. But when I built a reward system for listening, things improved dramatically! So treat yourself as you would someone you love. That grad-school application not coming along? Don't berate yourself or deprive yourself of sleep or playtime. Instead, reward yourself with something like an episode of *Orphan Black* for every question you complete. Love and respect yourself and you will flourish.

YOUR BREAKTHROUGH WORKSHEET

Try it with small challenges and build up to bigger ones.

TAKE AN IMPROV CLASS

WHY

I love to make people laugh and dream of being on *SNL*.

SCENARIO A
I stay in a job I don't like and wonder, What if?

SCENARIO B
I bomb. Comedy is out, but work presentations will be a breeze now.

SCENARIO C
I kill it! I'm on my way to achieving my dream.

REWARD FOR TAKING ACTION

A night out with people who make me laugh.

JULIE TOURETZKY, 22, was sobbing in her hospital bed as she tried to pass a kidney stone when the cosmic humor finally hit her. "It felt like a joke," Touretzky says. "How could this all be happening at once?"

Nothing in Touretzky's life seemed to be going right. First, the University of Delaware grad got back from studying abroad, and her relationship with her boyfriend ended abruptly. Less than a week later, during an interview for an internship, Touretzky was midsentence when the interviewer cut her off, telling her he couldn't tolerate listening to her talk. Between heartbreak, professional humiliation, and having to pee into a filter for a week, it was official: Touretzky's life sucked.

When Katherine Brown, 34, a government employee in Washington, D.C., bought her fixer-upper house in 2013, she entertained happy fantasies about the community she'd be joining

How to Deal When Your Life Explodes

Welcome to the Lifemageddon, when your life is full-on crumbling and the universe seems to be plotting against you. We've all been there. Here's how to get through it intact.

and the rose garden she would plant. In actuality, the yard was an irredeemable dirt patch littered with crack pipes. And the community? It played craps on her front stoop late into the night. Brown had to battle a rat problem and a bedbug infestation, which cost her thousands of dollars. Later, a pipe burst and flooded her basement. And in the midst of wrestling with her house problems, Brown applied for 35 jobs and was rejected by all of them. Finally, she got catfished on Match.com. She describes her streak of bad luck to be "almost hilarious."

However you look at it, you feel for these women, because you've been there too. At some point in our lives, we all go through a version of The Lifemageddon.

"Regular life is filled with traumatic events," says Mark Epstein, MD, a psychiatrist in New York City and author of *The Trauma of Everyday Life.* "And not just big ones like accidents and loss... difficult things happen every day." As life coach Gabrielle Bernstein, author of *Miracles Now: 108 Life-Changing Tools for Less Stress, More Flow, and Finding Your True Purpose*, puts it, "Everyone has had their dark night of the soul, their divine shitstorm." It's when the storm continues to pelt you that you wonder why it's happening...and what to do about it.

WHEN LIFEMAGEDDON STRIKES

There's no one way to react when you're hit with a series of unfortunate events. Lucy*, a 28-year-old actress in New York City, was "just crying all the time" during her Lifemageddon, she says.

She had good reason. Her father had been diagnosed with a rare form of cancer. One of her friends went into emergency surgery to have a brain tumor removed. Her boyfriend of four years broke up with her. And because he was also her boss, she had to quit her job. Even as the waterworks flowed, Lucy kept on with her life—going to the hospital gave her purpose. Then her dad got better and her friend woke up, but Lucy's state got worse.

No longer needing to visit the hospital, she stopped being able to get out of bed. She found excuses to drink heavily and dove into sexual relationships with two guy friends. "It was very rash but somehow felt therapeutic," Lucy says.

The behavior was risky but understandable. The actions Lucy took helped her "defend against the intolerable," as Dr. Epstein puts it. "It's hard to classify human responses as typical or atypical," says Christine Montross, MD, assistant professor of psychiatry and human behavior at Brown University and author of *Falling Into the Fire*. "It depends so much on the kinds of things we're facing and what strengths we bring to those situations."

For instance, when you find yourself overwhelmed by something challenging, you might lash out at your coworkers, play video games nonstop, or eat way too much. Or on the flip side, you might acknowledge right away that you're dealing with a difficult event and talk to friends, go to the gym, and get plenty of sleep.

Another common response is to turn away from the suffering altogether in order to protect yourself ("Stuff it down!" as Stephen Colbert says), because suffering hurts. But while turning away from the pain may be a knee-jerk reaction, it's not the best way to process. "You suffer less in the short-term, but it ends up hurting more because you're creating so much tension within yourself," Dr. Epstein says. That's what happened to Nancy Borowick, a 29-year-old photographer in New York City. She received a double dose of terrible news: her mother got her third diagnosis of breast cancer, then her father told her he had inoperable pancreatic cancer. "It was a massive shock to the system," she says.

Since her father didn't have much time, Borowick felt she had to get moving. She and her boyfriend of six years got engaged. The wedding happened 10 months later, and both her parents walked her down the aisle. Two months later, Borowick's father died. "I was doing a million different things that year, and I kept myself extremely busy. I didn't give myself a chance to crumble." But after she and her husband got back from their delayed honeymoon, Borowick finally did—in the middle of the airport. "It was like all of this finally became real, and I was going to be experiencing life without my dad." Her sadness and anxiety became debilitating, which is when Borowick was able to acknowledge that she needed to take care of herself. "I have taken a step back and am allowing myself to do what's best for me now."

MOVING FORWARD
In the midst of a Lifemageddon, look for relief from sources that fortify you.

"It's important to identify the things that are most healthy in our lives, so that when we hit periods of stress, we can automatically turn to those things," says Dr. Montross. Maybe you garden; maybe you run. Learning to practice meditation, starting therapy, and taking trapeze classes (yes) helped Borowick. Taking walks in the afternoon helped Lucy. Leaning on their networks of family and friends for support helped both of them.

But maybe you don't feel like you have a community nearby—you wouldn't be alone in feeling that way. In the last several decades, people have become less likely to be part of a club or a religious community or have close friends or family who live in their neighborhood, says David Campbell, PhD, director of the Rooney Center for the Study of American Democracy at the University of Notre Dame and coauthor of *American Grace: How*

WHAT'S BEHIND THE LIFEMAGEDDON?
When everything bad seems to happen at once, is it random, or does it mean more? Three experts assess.

"There are 7 billion people in the world. Somebody, somewhere, is just by chance going to have a few negative life events happen in quick succession. There's no mystical force. It's purely just chance."
—DAVID J. HAND, AUTHOR, *THE IMPROBABILITY PRINCIPLE*

Religion Divides and Unites Us. "When you're getting together with people on a regular basis, you get the sense that we're all in this together," Campbell says. Church, a support group, or a regular brunch with the same group of friends can become the safe place you need. "What's really helpful is for someone to sit with you and say, 'I really hear how awful this time is,'" says Dr. Montross.

It's also important to listen to your body. If you feel depleted, eat healthy food, go to bed earlier and find a way to take a day or two off work. If your initial response to a stressful situation is on the harmful side—whether you go on shopping sprees or hide, ignoring people's texts—try to recognize that. "The brain becomes practiced in dealing with negative events in certain ways, but you can change that if you pay attention to your patterns," says Meg Jay, PhD, a clinical assistant professor at the University of Virginia and author of *The*

Defining Decade: Why Your Twenties Matter—and How to Make the Most of Them Now.

Bad things don't necessarily produce silver linings, but if life really is this random, then chances are, good things will start to happen again. They did for Borowick, who photographed her parents during their treatment, and her work later catapulted her career. And Lucy landed a paid acting gig at a regional theater, where she bonded with a supportive community of colleagues. She still struggles sometimes, but she's had enough distance to reflect. "It's working on me in mysterious ways," she says. "I think that I've changed as a person."

Even though you'll probably never fully "get over" the events of your Lifemageddon, you'll come out wiser, says Dr. Epstein. "These traumas, these losses, they become us. We're seasoned by them."

THE PSYCHIATRIST SAYS

"Everyone goes through crises, and when you do, you have to make a distinction between responsibility and blame. Responsibility is realizing that even if you didn't cause your disaster, you can take actions to climb out of a bad place. Blame is counterproductive. Pointing the finger only makes things worse."
—MARK EPSTEIN, MD, AUTHOR, *THE TRAUMA OF EVERYDAY LIFE*

THE ASTROLOGER SAYS

"When life-changing experiences happen in a person's life, it could be a Saturn return, which draws out unresolved problems, or it could be the transit of an outer planet to a personal planet, which triggers changes. The disruptions and difficulties are intended to get us to clear out old emotional patterns that are not working in our life, so that we can finally reach our goals."
—COSMO ASTROLOGER AURORA TOWER

Let's Talk About Turning 30

Actress **Xosha Roquemore** (remember her from *The Mindy Project*?!) breaks down why all those things you should do/have/know by the time you're 30 are pretty bogus.

AS TOLD TO KATIE L. CONNOR

"**What I do recommend is a teddy nightgown. They're good for night sweats.**"

— XOSHA ROQUEMORE

AS TAMRA ON *THE MINDY PROJECT*, XOSHA BROUGHT THE ART OF THE ONE-LINER TO NEW HEIGHTS.

AROUND THE TIME YOU READ THIS, I will be 30. I'd like to say that I'm immune to the big-dealness of it, but I'm not. I thought I'd be wildly successful by 25! That wasn't true, but I realized I was on the right path. Say you want something at 25 and you get it at 32—is it any less sweet? No. Things come when they're supposed to and they're not any less of a milestone. The most important thing you should do or know by 30 is not to tell people what to do or know by 30. Here, some of the more egregious "shoulds" IMHO.

BY 30, YOU SHOULD KNOW...

...HOW TO FALL IN LOVE WITHOUT LOSING YOURSELF.

If you know how to do that, then you must have had a lot of experience with real, true love in your 20s! Me? I'm a late bloomer, so that doesn't make sense. For someone like me, who's had only two serious boyfriends, how would I know how to fall in love the right way?

...WHETHER OR NOT YOU WANT TO HAVE CHILDREN.

I'm super single—as are a lot of my friends. So having kids right now seems absolutely impossible and implausible. That's something so much bigger than you. To say you know exactly where you stand on it at 30? That's far too strict. Give yourself a break.

BY 30, YOU SHOULD HAVE...

...STOPPED BEING BOY CRAZY.

It's fun to be boy crazy; just don't act out. I totally lurk guys on social media, just to see what's out there. The other day, I found this guy on Instagram who was like a frickin' unicorn! He works in TV and he looks tall (I'm 5'10"). When you're single, it's nice to know that that unicorn is out there—that means there are others.

...A BLACK LACE BRA, CUSTOM-FITTED.

I have really small boobs. I need padding! Lace bras are too thin, so I can't imagine they're a great investment for bigger chests either. What I do recommend is a teddy nightgown. They're good for night sweats. By 30, you may discover you have a new tendency to sweat in bizarre places. I'm like, oh hell, why do I have a vagina pit stain? Put that cash toward a nightie instead.

Get Inspired to Succeed

Nine amazing ideas to spark your creativity, up your mojo, and make things happen.

1

THRIVE!

"My secret to feeling I can do anything I need to do is giving my body the food, exercise, water, and sleep it needs."

—CAMERON DIAZ, ACTRESS, AUTHOR, *THE BODY BOOK*

2

DREAM

"I have a sick love of being in over my head at all times! I never want to play it safe. I love taking familiar flavors that folks already know and turning them upside down—like cereal milk becoming ice cream or apple pie becoming a layer cake! I try to think honestly about what I love to eat and then find imaginative ways to share it."

—CHRISTINA TOSI, CHEF, FOUNDER, AND OWNER OF MOMOFUKU MILK BAR

3

WORK OUT

"Figure out what your power place is, the place or thing or memory that makes you truly happy. For me, it's my hometown beach on the east end of Long Island. Once you figure out your specific power place, you can use it to create a more positive association for working out. Next time you go to work out, close your eyes and bring your power place to life. Mix it up, and make it fast. Avoiding a workout because you dread mind-numbing cardio is no longer an excuse. Try CosmoBody or another platform that provides a big mix of types and durations of workouts, and you'll always have whatever sounds good at any given moment at your fingertips."

—ADAM ROSANTE, COSMOBODY TRAINER

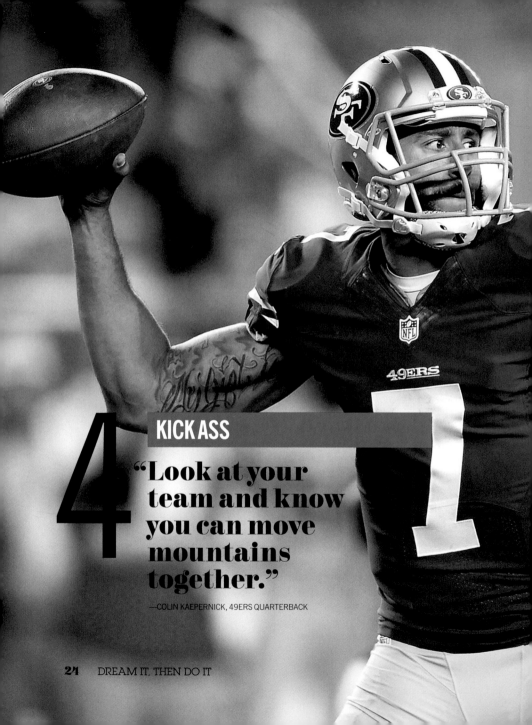

4 KICK ASS

"Look at your team and know you can move mountains together."

—COLIN KAEPERNICK, 49ERS QUARTERBACK

Veronica Roth (left) and
Shailene Woodley (right)

5 GROW

"You don't get better without criticism. As a writer, I need honest feedback about my work to make my writing better. I learned that in college. One of my professors kept pushing me to write more honestly, and the voice of Tris [the heroine of Roth's blockbuster *Divergent* trilogy] really developed as a reaction to that. I still work with critique partners, and that's only valuable if you don't get defensive. Part of being a professional is about getting over it, meaning you have to separate yourself from your work and realize that if someone is criticizing your writing, they're not criticizing you. I am a bigger, more complicated person than any book. Every human being is a crazy festival of thoughts. You have to have a life outside your work."

—VERONICA ROTH, AUTHOR, *DIVERGENT* SERIES

6 BREAK OUT

"I'm constantly trying to expose myself to new things, because I'm always working in my head. The cool thing about inspiration is that you can't just say, 'This is what I'm going to be inspired by today.' Instead, it's about alerting your senses and seeing what sticks. I do things that please my eyeballs by looking at beautiful things, like the produce at a farmers' market. I find value in messy, loud social-media sources, like Instagram, as well as from reading more serious business magazines."

—SOPHIA AMORUSO, NASTY GAL

7 BE POSITIVE 😃

"Your inner mentor is that part inside you that is wise and secure. Learn to listen to her, rather than your inner critic, the voice of self-doubt. That's the first major step toward playing bigger, aka trusting and expressing your voice and pursuing your aspirations."

—TARA MOHR, AUTHOR, *PLAYING BIG*

8 CHANGE THINGS UP

"It's hard to have creativity in a vacuum, so I put together a mix of activities that will expose you to things outside your comfort zone. They should make you more curious about everything around you." Try these:

READ (or watch or listen to) the same story as covered by three news sources from different points on the political spectrum. How much did the coverage differ?

DRAW A SELF-PORTRAIT every day for 30 consecutive days. At the end of that time, think about how your portraits evolved.

WALK OR DRIVE A DIFFERENT PATH to work or school every day for a week. At the end, list the new things you saw.

—ALEX EGNER, AUTHOR OF *EXPERIENCE PASSPORT* AND A PROFESSOR AT THE UNIVERSITY OF NORTH TEXAS

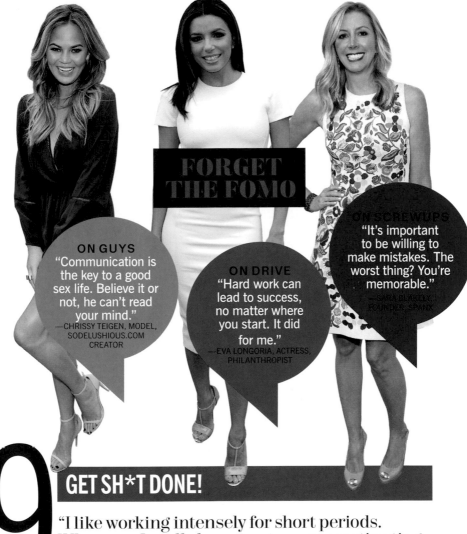

FORGET THE FOMO

ON GUYS
"Communication is the key to a good sex life. Believe it or not, he can't read your mind."
—CHRISSY TEIGEN, MODEL, SODELUSHIOUS.COM CREATOR

ON DRIVE
"Hard work can lead to success, no matter where you start. It did for me."
—EVA LONGORIA, ACTRESS, PHILANTHROPIST

ON SCREWUPS
"It's important to be willing to make mistakes. The worst thing? You're memorable."
—SARA BLAKELY, FOUNDER, SPANX

9

GET SH*T DONE!

"I like working intensely for short periods. Whenever I really have to stop procrastinating and be productive, I tweet that I'm doing a 'writing sprint' and invite everyone to join me by working on whatever they have to do. People are always like 'I'm in!' The sense of community and obligation that engenders is empowering! You'll be amazed what you can accomplish."

—JANE ESPENSON, CONSULTING PRODUCER, ABC'S *ONCE UPON A TIME*

27

Do You Trust Your Gut?

Is your gut ready for a life change?

1.

That little voice inside you:

A. Says of course you can wear that white bodycon dress from Nasty Gal to your sister's wedding!

B. Justifies spending your rent on a lock of Harry Styles' hair on eBay. It's an investment. One day, he'll be shiny-head bald.

C. Is a loop of your greatest fears: sharks, intimacy, cellulite, dying alone....

2.

Your BF proposes and you promptly feel sick. Clearly, this means you should:

A. Run for it! Love shouldn't feel like the day after a Four Loko bender in TJ when you wake up on the beach wearing a full banana costume and heels.

B. Consult your horoscope. If he has a Gemini moon rising, blame it on the saag paneer you ate at lunch.

C. Say yes to the dress! All your friends are married—it's your turn, betch!

3.

You're at a soul-sucking job with no room for growth. You:

A. Quit cold-turkey and sell your eggs.

B. Start letting strangers braid your hair for $40 a pop on Craigslist. Hey, it's a living.

C. Prepare to sacrifice your youth in the hopes that one day this dumb job will pay off and you'll become the greatest part-time night receptionist in debt-collection agency history.

4.

You buy a facial on Groupon, but when you get to the "salon," it's just a fold-out table in an abandoned meat factory. You:

A. Demand a refund and Yelp the crap out of that place.

B. Blurt an excuse. "I forgot to feed my diabetic chinchilla, Morris! He'll have a seizure if he doesn't get his night worms. BRB!"

C. Take a Valium, lie back, and just remember it's all fodder for your memoir, *Eat, Save, Groupon: A Cheap Woman's Journey.*

5.

Your dream is to be a visual artist, but your parents want you to do something practical. You decide to:

A. Follow your bliss to Marfa, live in an Airstream, and wear hella turquoise.

B. Become a painter...with a day job. No one needs to know about your bar mitzvah DJ side hustle.

C. Stop painting and ease into the spicy world of data entry. There's an opening at TelAmeriCorps!

MOSTLY A'S
Angelina Jolie

Like Angie J during the '90s, you are a wild woman who follows every hunch, no matter the consequences. While listening to your gut is good, there are other things to listen to, such as reason, logic, Newton's law of gravity, Beyoncé... hell, even your mom, once in a while. Keep doing you, but maybe look a couple of seconds longer before you leap.

MOSTLY B'S
Gwen Stefani

Like this superstar, you stay true to yourself. Sure, you've made mistakes, mostly involving bindis and sports bras as formal wear, but you're only human! You have the right combo of following your dreams but also not having stupid dreams. Bravo!

MOSTLY C'S
Lindsay Lohan

You just got a text from your gut: "Stop ignoring me!" The way you live is like an avant-garde art experiment: Let's do the opposite of what feels right all the time. What would your life be like if you stopped listening to what everyone else thinks? Spoiler alert: Awesome.

Anxiety Attack Hacks

Having a moment?! No worries. These tricks will stop your freak-out in its tracks.

1. YOU'RE RUNNING LATE

This seems like a super-frustrating sitch that you have no control over—which, TBH, it kind of is—but it's not so bad! "Your own thoughts, like this traffic is endless or my boss will flip, often cause stress," says Greta Hirsch, PhD, clinical director of the Ross Center for Anxiety. "Your brain is confusing possibility with probability."

TRY THIS: Drown out negative messages by listening to a playlist you find engrossing. Better still: Sing along. "When we use our vocal cords, it sends a signal to our brain that we're okay," says Kelli Walker, RN, a panic and anxiety coach.

2. YOU CAN'T SLEEP

First, don't look at the clock. Watching minutes tick by creates the opposite physical response (a rush of adrenaline and cortisol, rapid heart beat, and sweating) of the relaxation you need to doze off, Hirsch says. Second, don't grab your phone or Kindle. "Screens cue our brains to get up and get moving," says Walker.

TRY THIS: Instead of fighting it, accept that you're not sleeping but you are resting, and meditate on how awesome that is. Suggests Hirsch: "Take deep breaths as you repeat thoughts like my bed is delicious, I love the feel of my blanket, it's quiet."

3. YOU'RE IN A SPAT

Fights with a BF or BFF can easily escalate from mildly distracting to all-consuming since our instinct is to overanalyze. "Don't equate not calling with not caring—maybe he's in a meeting, maybe she's sleeping in," says Hirsch. "It just sends your anxiety up and your mood down."

TRY THIS: Assign a specific worry window. "Take a walk with a coworker, and make that the 15 minutes when you focus on the issue," Hirsch suggests. "Then, that's it." Not only does activity expend energy, but a scenery change helps you associate your desk with work time once you're back.

4. YOU'RE NERVOUS

When your hands are shaking before an interview or your heart is racing pre–first date, remember that anxiety isn't just normal in these situations, it's good. "Anxiety motivates us," says Hirsch. "Otherwise, we wouldn't prepare; we'd show up in gym clothes."

TRY THIS: Literally chill out: For a few minutes, dip your hands in cold water or hold a cool drink on your tongue. "This triggers the vagus nerve, which signals the body to calm down," says Walker. Now go crush it.

Shake Off the Haters

It's easy to get sucked down a despair spiral after a nasty comment on your Instagram or Twitter feed. Stop! We got advice from people who have been there on how to keep it all in perspective.

"Step away from it. I have thousands, maybe millions, of positive social-media comments, but if I see something negative, I'm upset. So I reaffirm to myself that I'm not what this person, who doesn't know me, says. Talking it through with a friend really helps too."

—LAVERNE COX, ACTRESS, *ORANGE IS THE NEW BLACK*

"I look through what else a troll is posting. Often, they're baiting anybody they think will answer. That helps me realize how impersonal it is and helps me to stop replying!"

—MEG CABOT, AUTHOR, *ROYAL WEDDING*

"At first, I was dramatic about people being hateful about my writing and my weight. Now, it's almost kind of funny. Sometimes I'll read a colorful insult and think, that's terrible, but wow, you got creative there!"

—ANNA TODD, AUTHOR, THE *AFTER* SERIES

"Responding mires you in the negativity, which is unhealthy. Even if I have a valid defense for whatever I'm being attacked on, the people who don't like me won't believe it, so there's no point in getting pulled in."

—MEGYN KELLY, FOX NEWS ANCHOR AND HOST, *THE KELLY FILE*

"I made the mistake once of taking sides on who Elena, my *Vampire Diaries* character, should end up with. It was like putting a target on my head! But it goes to show that no matter what you say, someone's going to be unhappy. Tell yourself that social media is like high school for adults—but worse—and get over it."

—NINA DOBREV, ACTRESS, *THE VAMPIRE DIARIES*

"I'm getting hit hard over my female *Ghostbusters* reboot. But if I fire something back, I'm giving the haters an audience. Being small-minded is their cross to bear. I won't fall down into their world—it's not as nice as mine."

—PAUL FEIG, DIRECTOR, *SPY*

Show Off Your Best Self

HI, I'M ALIZA LICHT. It's great to meet you. Welcome to my career crash course.

Leave your mark by honing your message, raising your social profile, and nailing your signature style. It's time to act, dress, and tweet like a boss.

As DKNY PR Girl, the voice behind @dkny on Twitter and the SVP of Global Communications at Donna Karan International, I have had the privilege of sharing my insider views on the glamorous, and sometimes not so glamorous, world of fashion in 140 characters or less.

Whether I'm tweeting about Oscar gowns that have gone missing at LAX or the ridiculous fashion-show ticket requests that come into my inbox, my tweets offer a juicy behind-the-scenes peek at fashion through the lens of public relations. But something interesting happened since I started DKNY PR Girl in 2009: Social media has also become a vehicle for me to mentor.

Take this example of a blogger named Jenna who I got to know through Twitter. She direct-messaged me one day asking if she could e-mail a few questions. She told me that she worked at an artificial turf manufacturing company but she loved fashion. I responded by simply writing, "Call me."

I had a lot of advice, and the bottom line was that if she wanted to break into fashion, she needed to be in New York. Sigh. I knew Jenna hung up the phone with a heavy heart and a swirling head.

alizalichtxo

Follow

· PEOPLE ·
LOVE
· TO BE ·
INSPIRED

n Thank

Months later when Jenna called again and told me she'd packed up and moved to New York, I couldn't help but be impressed. She had taken our conversation seriously. She was hungry.

Jenna had been working at a PR agency in New York for six months when I started a search for a new assistant. Since I was looking for someone socially savvy, I asked the applicants to apply on DKNY's Facebook page. We received 300 applications, including one from Jenna. People treated the process like they behave socially—very casually. But they shouldn't have. I wanted to see if the applicants were savvy enough to know how to switch between social talk and professional communication. Jenna intuitively knew the difference. After a long, drawn-out process, Jenna was the one. One tweet from a girl at an artificial turf company in Texas led to her dream job in fashion in New York City.

Jenna's clear talent and instinct to behave in the professional way she did made me want to help her. And that brings me to the biggest secret I've learned: How you communicate and influence others weighs just as heavily on your success as your skills and ideas do. When you spend all day strategizing how to make people perceive a brand positively like I do, you start to realize that the same principles can be applied to people.

My knowledge comes from nearly 20 years of experience, but I want to give you a cheat sheet on how to market yourself. Why wait to learn something the hard way when I can teach you now?

1. DEFINE YOUR
PERSONAL BRAND

What is a brand? It's an identity. Branding is the art of aligning what you want people to think about you with what people actually think about you. You can decide what you want the public perception of you to be, and you can shape it. So the question is: How would your friends or colleagues describe you? Is that the message you want to convey? If it's not, you need to change it. You need to self-examine and decide what you want to stand for. Every person has something unique to offer. To know what that is, look at yourself from an outsider's point of view.

CRAFT YOUR PERSONAL BRAND.

Pretend for a moment that you are a public relations executive and your new client is you. Answer the following questions.
Who are you?
What makes you special?

What do people remember most after meeting you?

WRITE YOUR BIO. Do a summary of you—your professional and personal life—in the third person, which allows you to take a step back and not feel totally awkward talking about yourself. Pretend you're a journalist who is writing an article about you for the *New York Times*. Throw it all in there: your looks, personality, education, job titles, hobbies, passions, talents, awards, charity work, and family life.

READ YOUR BIO. Cozy up somewhere, and pretend you're reading about someone else. Do you like this person? Are you impressed by what she's done? What do you feel this person should change about herself?

MAKE A WORD CLOUD. Pull the keywords in your bio that really summarize your story.

CREATE A MOOD BOARD. Find an image for each word you pulled out. Take a step back. What do you want to keep? What do you want to change?

CONTINUE THE STORY. Think about where you want your journey to go. Continue writing your bio as if it has happened, but this time in italics—all your aspirations, everything you want to accomplish. This may sound like a lot of work and soul-searching—and it is.

But when you're finished, you will know yourself so much better. Personal branding is about identifying the best version of you. It will allow you to perform better in every area of your life, no matter what you do.

2. KILL IT ON
SOCIAL MEDIA

Social media has helped catapult seemingly regular people into personal brands. Hello, you're reading the words of someone who is a product of social media. What you post speaks volumes about you. That can be a good or bad thing. Just remember, when you're at a party this big, you better bring your manners—your personal brand depends on it.

FIND THE PLATFORM—AND THE NUMBER OF PLATFORMS—THAT FEELS RIGHT FOR YOU. You don't need to be everywhere. Master one or two platforms first, and grow from there.

Plan your strategy on the kind of content you have to work with. For example, if you're not really going to have strong visual assets, consider skipping Instagram until you do.

THE PROFILE PICTURE AND BIO IN SOCIAL MEDIA ARE LIKE YOUR RÉSUMÉ. Don't leave them blank.

POSTING AND ENGAGING WITH YOUR FOLLOWERS REGULARLY WILL GROW YOUR FOLLOWING. You have to start the conversation and follow the conversation. Out of sight, out of mind strongly applies here.

LISTEN BEFORE YOU SPEAK. Growing up, we were told to think before we speak. In social media, you need to listen (i.e., read). Know what conversations people are having before you chime in.

SCRATCH PEOPLE'S BACKS. When you can't think of anything original to post, try helping others get their thoughts out there. Giving voice to other people's posts by sharing them is a gracious move and one that's always returned in spades. It's also a great way to build your follower base.

EMBRACE YOURSELF. The truer you are to yourself, the happier you'll be anyway. If you love to cook, for example, share some fun tips that position you as an expert. If you're someone who loves staying home and watching movies, why not become your own movie critic and post reviews socially? There are a lot of ways to prove your worth, and providing some kind of service to your followers is always a great tactic.

DON'T BEG. Do you beg for friends in real life? I doubt it. So why would you beg for friends online? How you build a follower base is the result of three things: (1) putting out great content, (2) engaging with people who speak to you, and (3) proactively reaching out to others.

STRIKE UP A CONVERSATION ONLINE. Ask someone a smart question, or compliment something he has recently accomplished.

INSPIRE! People love to be inspired. That's why quotes, whether motivational or encouraging, go a long way in the social space. Quotes are pretty much a given to be retweeted, which will grow your audience exponentially.

CURATE YOUR TIMELINE. Retweeting five times in a row might give off the idea that you don't post original content. I believe in an eclectic timeline. Start with posting original content, then respond to some comments, and finally share other people's content. You want to show that you are both speaking and watching the various conversations throughout the day. Check your timeline once in a while, and see if you think it would look good to someone who doesn't know you.

Filter what you say. If you wouldn't feel comfortable running a full-page ad of your tweet in the *New York Times*, don't post it.

3. CREATE YOUR
OWN LOOK

I once had a very open conversation with a stylist friend who wanted to put his client in Donna Karan New York for a movie premiere. Celeb X wanted to be fresh, relatable, all American. "That's why we're not putting her in European designers anymore," he said. "She's the chic girl next door." Just like that, Celeb X's new style image was born. Style is one factor in creating your personal brand, and it's probably the easiest way to reinvent yourself. You may think that having a strong sense of personal style doesn't matter for what you want to do, but I promise you that it leads to confidence in other more important areas. Your style needs to empower you to take on the world each day. That's what fashion does for me. It gives me the energy and confidence to tackle whatever comes my way. Well, that and coffee.

KNOW YOUR BODY! Certain styles look better for your shape than others do. Don't convince yourself that you should be able to wear everything.

GET STYLE-INSPIRED. Gather images of people whose style you most admire. Try to find the common denominators.

RECORD BEST OUTFITS. Believe it or not, a good style moment can be forgotten in a nanosecond. If you find a great look that made you feel wonderful, write it down, or better yet, photograph it.

STORE YOUR GO-TO CLOTHES TOGETHER. These are the pieces that never let you down. The pants that fit no matter what you ate that week. The shirt that never wrinkles. When you are pressed for time, you want easy access to the items that work.

HANG BY LOOK. If you're organized, keep some of your important looks together. It helps immensely in saving you time and helping you remember what that great outfit is.

KEEP YOUR JOB IN MIND. No matter how much fun you want to have with your style, do remember the job you have.

IDENTIFY A SIGNATURE ITEM. Repetition is reputation. For me, it's the red lipstick and red nails.

ADAPTED FROM *LEAVE YOUR MARK*, BY ALIZA LICHT, GRAND CENTRAL PUBLISHING.

KILL the NEG-A-THON

What makes a fun night out descend into a competitive, self-shaming festival of woe? Life coach and motivational speaker Gabrielle Bernstein, author of *Miracles Now*, helps you break the cycle.

You're finishing off a slice of crazy good pie with your three BFFs—one dessert, four forks—when it happens again: "God, I can't believe I ate so much. I feel so fat." No matter who says it first or how much fun you've been having, it's almost inevitable that someone else will chime in: "I haven't been to the gym all week! My thighs are rubbing together." Everyone groans in sympathy and you're off, recounting diet sins and self-deprecating stories, each upping the ante until the sweetness of the evening (never mind the chocolate) fades, and you all end up going home feeling as if Girls' Night Out was kind of a bummer.

Why does this always happen? Partly, I think it's the fact that in our culture, women are taught that it's nicer to see ourselves as deficient than to brag about our accomplishments. The female brain is also hardwired for connection. We want to share any discomfort and pain we're experiencing so we don't feel so alone.

The trouble is, cataloging your flaws with your besties will only take you to a dark place.

So what to do when the night veers into downer territory? Saying "Hey, guys, can we talk about something else?" isn't necessarily the solution in this case, because it implies that your friends are wrong, which might cause friction. Try these tiny mental tools to refocus the conversation in a more subtle way.

WAIT When you're tempted to join the negging, think WAIT, as in Why Am I Talking? Pause to ask yourself what kind of connection you're seeking or what bad feeling you're trying to soothe. Then let yourself feel the emotions by breathing in for 90 seconds. Once you realize, Oh, that's what this is about, those thoughts will usually drift away.

LEAD Think of yourself as a sort of conversation healer. Try to shift the group's energy from draining to uplifting. Give a non-looks-related compliment ("Your new job sounds exciting!"), or share some positive news ("I'm planning a Mexico vacay. Any tips?"). Redirect the flow of words to higher ground.

SNAP Every time you see a quote or picture that makes you feel good about life, snap a screenshot and save it in a special album on your phone. Flash one to the group when the chatting starts to go dark. If all else fails, inspiring kitten pics to the rescue!

PEACE OUT Press your pointer finger to your thumb, then do the same with your middle finger, ring finger, and pinkie, saying with each touch to the thumb, "Peace. Begins. With. Me." It's a combo mantra and mudra (a Buddhist name for hand gesture) you can use anywhere. The phrase gets you into a calmer headspace, and the mudra sends messages to your brain, like a mini acupressure. The pointer finger releases wisdom, the middle, patience (something to remind yourself of when you're tempted to flip someone the bird), the ring finger, knowledge, and the pinkie, vision and inspiration.

2
WORK & MONEY

DRESS FOR THE JOB YOU WANT

These women want to make a big career change—and they asked **Cosmo** for a style makeover to get them started. Their future begins...now!

"I WANT TO SOLVE CRIMES"

NAME: Zalika Paul, 28
DREAM JOB: Police Detective

"I feel the need to help people. Solving crimes would be so rewarding. I'm always working on solutions to problems, and I'm passionate about criminal justice."

ZALIKA'S POWER LOOK

Zalika works in a conservative industry (she's usually in uniform!), but she also loves fashion. She can't go wrong with a skirt and blouse topped with a blazer to show that she means business. But the chic print of the top and bold color and shape of the skirt let her express some style. The structured blue bag can fit everything Zalika needs while adding a fun nod to her personality.

As for makeup, all Zalika needs is a matte foundation that evens her complexion and two coats of a standard black mascara to bring out her eyes. For hair, a strong-hold styling spray tames flyaways and boosts shine in this pulled-back, sleek style.

Blazer, **NYDJ**®. *Shirt,* **Calvin Klein**®. *Skirt,* **Eloquii**®. *Shoes,* **French Connection**®. *Bag,* **Kate Spade**®. *Saturday Earrings,* **Lydell NYC**®

Alterna Pieces

A trench coat is a must for any detective. Coat, **LE TRENCH**®

The red color gives this classic button-down some flair. Shirt, **VINCE**®

Communicate power in this simple black skirt with a white stripe. Skirt, **XOXO**®

A heel with a feminine shape and modest height is stylish but practical. Shoes, **BANANA REPUBLIC**®

"I WANT MY OWN COOKING SHOW"

NAME: Yasmin Elgibali
DREAM JOB: Cooking-Show Host

"I would love to do a show where I visit real people in their kitchens and cook meals that work for their lifestyles. I want to look effortlessly chic."

YASMIN'S POWER LOOK

Since she needs to roll up her sleeves to make her meals, Yasmin's clothes can't be precious. The shapes are simple and practical while playing with textured materials and pops of color to add personality. For a go-to day makeup look, we gave Yasmin a smoky eye, keeping the darkest colors close to the lash line. And a braid with thickening spray keeps her hair smooth and contained.

Sweater, **SACHIN & BABI**®.
Pants, **CRIPPEN**®. *Shoes,* **DIESEL**®.
Bag, **FRENCH CONNECTION**®.
All jewelry, **WHITE MOTH JEWELRY**®

"I WANT TO BE A FASHION MARKETER"

NAME: Ashley Small
DREAM JOB: Fashion Marketing

"Before college, I spent five years in the Navy as a fiber-optics engineer, saving up for school. I loved the camaraderie, but there's nothing like taking off your steel-toe boots at the end of the day and putting on shoes you love. I've always wanted to work in marketing. It's the quickest way to tell a story and change people's lives."

ASHLEY'S POWER LOOK

Your goal on a job interview is to let the real you show through, so Ashley was excited to rock a chic Afro.

"A touch of finishing cream keeps the look polished," says Cosmo executive beauty director Leah Wyar. Adds executive fashion director Aya Kanai, "When you're interviewing for a fashion-marketing job, you want to show that you're professional and on-trend. This crisp white shirt has a clever tail, which gives a nice twist to a pulled-together look. And the bright pumps add just the right amount of color." And since Ashley won't need to play it safe in the fashion industry, makeup pro Melissa Silver used a bold emerald shadow to make her eyes pop. The rest of the look is clean, with a creamy nude lip.

Blazer and shirt, **KENNETH COLE®**. *Pants,* **NEW YORK AND COMPANY®**. *Shoes,* **KATE SPADE®** **NEW YORK**. *Bag,* **THE LIMITED®**. *Earrings,* **REBECCA MINKOFF**

Bold color and subtle details
catch the eye without looking
busy. Sweater, **REBECCA TAYLOR**®

Alterna
Pieces

Use the handles when you're
feeling proper—and the strap
when you're hauling ass.
Bag, **KATE SPADE**® **NEW YORK**

Leather is both comfy and edgy
at the same time. Skirt,
C/MEO COLLECTIVE®

For big
meetings,
sturdy heels
make a stror
impression.
Shoes, **GX BY
GWEN STEFANI**®

"I WANT TO BE IN PHARMA SALES"

NAME: Paige Yurick
DREAM JOB: Pharmaceutical Sales Rep

"Ever since I was little, I wanted to be a doctor. But as a biology major at Villanova, I realized I didn't want to be in school forever and then have so much debt. I also realized I wanted to be able to help a lot of people. As a sales rep who talks to doctors about new drugs that could help patients, I'd have the potential do that."

PAIGE'S POWER LOOK

Polished waves are ideal for a job in a relatively conservative industry like pharma, says Wyar. Wrap hair around a 1.5" curling iron, brush through, and apply a dab of smoothing cream to add shine. For a natural, pretty makeup look that's easy to touch up in between sales calls, Silver used a sheer red-orange lip hue, then she defined Paige's eyes with neutral shadow, crisp liner, and two coats of black mascara. And since sales is about relationships, you want to show your personality, advises Kanai. A modern pantsuit and slingback heels do it while keeping you corporate-ready.

Jacket and pants, **ANN TAYLOR**®. *Blouse,* **JONES NEW YORK**®. *Belt,* **JOE FRESH**®. *Shoes,* **IVANKA TRUMP**®. *Bag,* **DOONEY AND BOURKE**®. *Necklace,* **BAR III**®. *Bracelet,* **HEARTS ON FIRE**®

Why You Need a Go-To Look

Celebrities have their signature beauty styles. Could one help you at work?

WHAT DO LAUREN CONRAD and Kim Kardashian West have in common? Both have been building their brands using their ambition, charisma, and one very subtle strategy: a signature beauty look. Don't think of it as just hair and makeup—think of it as your professional PR.

1 It Says You're Trustworthy

"Consistency—even in your look—makes people trust you. It sends an unspoken message that you can be counted on," says Laurin Sydney, who coaches people for public appearances. "If you go to work with a bare face on Monday and aqua shadow the next, it creates the perception you're spending too much time experimenting with your look, not focusing on work," she says. Sydney admits it's unfair, often inaccurate, but "at work, perception is reality."

2 It's a Visual Promotion

Keeping your beauty game tight also conveys maturity. "Experimenting with your identity can appear like you're an adolescent," says Vivian Diller, PhD, a psychologist who specializes in women's issues.

"It's assumed that as an adult, you know yourself, your values, and your look." Take Victoria Beckham: After playing the glammed soccer wife (with spiky pixies and extensions in between), now she maintains a trademark bob to match her critically acclaimed fashion career.

3 It Gives You Star Quality

"A beauty signature creates a way for people to remember you," says Diller. It doesn't have to shout—Jennifer Aniston has made the natural look her thing for a decade-plus!—just be consistent. If this evokes a fear of living a beauty Groundhog Day, relax. A beauty signature can still have range. If you're a bold-lip girl, try peony one day, poppy the next. If you're working a lob, go sleek on Thursday, shaggy on Friday. As Sydney says, "Be creative within the bounds of your trademark style!"

EASY WAYS TO MAKE A STATEMENT
Attention grabbing, yet work-appropriate

POWER BROW
Strong arches add instant sophistication.
ANASTASIA BEVERLY HILLS® *Perfect Brow Pencil in Dark Brown, sephora.com*

AN ORANGE LIP
More fun than red, with just as much impact.
RIMMEL MOISTURE RENEW® *Lipstick in In Love With Ginger, drugstores .com*

NAVY LINER
A chic upgrade from ho-hum black.
LANCÔME ARTLINER® *in Navy, lancome.com*

DEWY SKIN
Make a glow-y complexion your thing.
LAURA MERCIER® *Tinted Moisturizer Illuminating,* **SEPHORA®**

—ZOOEY DESCHANEL IS RARELY SEEN WITHOUT HER TRADEMARK BANGS.

Does Your Hair Work for Work?

Every morning before work, tons of curly-haired women straighten their hair. Some love the look; others feel the pressure. **Anna Breslaw** explores workplace hair bias.

IN YOUR AVERAGE workplace rom-com, the boss is a Katherine Heigl–ish, type-A workaholic whose stick-straight hair is as indicative of her competence as her four-inch black stilettos. Curly-haired girls like me? We're not usually in those roles. Instead, we're playing second fiddle to real stars (cue Judy Greer's Penny to J.Lo's Mary in *The Wedding Planner*), waiting to be made over (à la *Clueless*)... or making an ass of ourselves on the job (*Never Been Kissed*). In Hollywood, curly hair just isn't taken that seriously at work.

For me, real life isn't much different. At my first office job, I found myself in a crowded elevator, the sole ringletted head among straight locks. If there were other curly girls, they concealed it with perfect Kate Middleton–esque blowouts.

While my curls were quirky—a conversation piece at parties ("How often do you have to wash it? Does everyone in your family have it? Are you [insert taste-less ethnicity question here]?")—they just felt out of place (even inappropriate) in straitlaced office culture. I wish I could say I was the only one who felt this way.

Marla, 25, recalls getting some unsolicited advice after one of her post-collegiate job interviews didn't end with an offer. "She asked, 'What were you thinking wearing your hair curly for an interview?'"

When Michelle Breyer started reporting business news for a local TV station, she quickly learned her curls weren't camera-friendly. "The first day on the job, I got called into my producer's office, who said, 'We need to do something about your hair.'" Shortly after that experience, Michelle founded NaturallyCurly.com, which has become the largest social-media platform and resource for women with textured or curly hair.

Midge Wilson, PhD, a professor

of psychology and women's and gender studies at DePaul University, says it wasn't always this way.

"The '60s were tolerant of curly hair among whites as well as the Afro for African-Americans and Jews," she says. "It seemed loose, free-spirited, even wild." Once the Free Love era was over, that perception became a prejudice. "In pop culture, deranged women often have big, uncombed curls. Well-groomed hair is seen as no-nonsense and serious."

Consider the case of Florida Congresswoman Debbie Wasserman Schultz, who is well known for her natural curls. A 2012 *Vogue* piece on Wasserman Schultz referred to her as frizzy-haired yet ran an accompanying photo of her with a blowout. "Many who know Wasserman Schultz called the picture unrecognizable," noted a recent Politico article. Chelsea Clinton spent her adolescence mocked on *SNL* for her unruly curls. As an adult, she adopted an immaculate blonde blowout, and the snickering stopped.

For black women, the curly hair stigma is even more problematic. For two years, Brooke, 25, was devoted to what she calls "the creamy crack"—a chemical straightening treatment that takes more than three hours, costs $200 or more, and must be done every two months or so. The process, she said, was hell. "The chemicals feel like they're burning into the depths of your very soul." Ultimately, she went back to her natural texture—a subject thoroughly chronicled in Chris Rock's 2009 HBO documentary *Good Hair*, which showed this landscape to be a complex issue that resonates way outside the office.

Just as Chris was critiquing one form of hair torture, another pricey (although less painful) hair ritual was on the rise: the professional blowout. DreamDry, Drybar, and similar niche salons count many working women as customers. But at about $40 a pop, you have to make bank to splurge on them. Some women view this as an operational expense. "I make very little money, yet I'm required to look professional every day," says Dana, 28.

And the humidity avoidance factor: I avoided the water on beach trips and planned (or skipped) workouts based on my hair. And If I stepped out of the salon after springing for a blowout and it was drizzling? I was screwed. Of course, when you're trying to be taken seriously at work, these seem like small sacrifices. As a nervous college grad, racing to interviews, I was convinced nixing my curls would make me look more capable, so I routinely turned up my straightener to the highest setting and ended up frying my strands, root to tip.

In retrospect, I'm sad for the girl I was then—and not just because I had

fried hair for months. So after spending my energy trying to perfect a smooth, polished style, I finally figured out how to work with what I have. And recently, when my younger sister wanted to flatiron her curls for a job interview, I steered her toward curl-centric products instead. (My favorites: Ouidad Climate Control Heat & Humidity Gel and Moisture Lock Leave-In Conditioner, ouidad.com.)

So own your natural style, corporate women. Hell, throw in a big old hair toss for good measure. If everyone stopped straightening just to be taken seriously, it would be pretty obvious that curly hair can mean totally capable.

Be More Creative Every Day

Looking for office inspiration? Paramount Pictures' **Amy Powell**, president of the studio's TV arm, digital entertainment, and Insurge Pictures, has tons of ideas.

1 ALWAYS BE EXPLORING

To be creative, you have to remain curious. Travel! Explore new places, meet new people, try new foods. Immerse yourself in culture. Go to the movies opening weekend; follow artists, fashion, and friends on Instagram; binge-watch television; visit a museum; experience live music; and read voraciously.

2 GET OUT OF YOUR COMFORT ZONE

Try to avoid falling into a rigid schedule. Routine leads to familiarity and complacency, which leads to a lack of passion and creativity. I like to challenge my team to meet in different spaces and vary the agenda from week to week. Small changes—inviting a different colleague to coffee once a week or taking a quick walk with a coworker—can stimulate you to think in new ways.

3 TAKE TIME TO RIFF

Throughout my career, I've had one weekly meeting with no agenda but to talk about what's happening in the zeitgeist, interesting articles, and passion points. It allows people to feed off one another— we'll often take a small idea and turn it into something big.

4 CHAT UP A STRANGER

When I throw a dinner party, I purposely sit people next to people they don't know. I get so excited when I sit down with somebody who is thinking of traveling to a place off the beaten path or learning to speak Italian. I once met someone on an airplane and ended up hiring her four years later!

5 PUT AWAY YOUR PHONE

My mother always says, "Don't forget to stop and smell the roses." Well, it's hard to smell the roses if your face is glued to your phone. Try to log off and notice the world around you every now and again. I am always surprised by the ideas that germinate when my phone is firmly placed at the bottom of my purse.

6 HELP OTHERS

Giving back is probably the best way to combine all these tips in one. Find a charity that resonates with you personally and that needs your help. It doesn't have to be hugely ambitious—do a little something that makes you feel connected to the things that matter most to you. A little step could lead to a big involvement later in your life.

Find Work That Feels Like Play

Everyone says do what you love, but what if you have no idea what that is? **Caitlin Moran**—39-year-old novelist, TV writer, and columnist for *The Times of London*—can help.

VISUALIZE YOUR FUTURE

If you are having trouble breaking in, read everything you can about the place where you would like to work. Think about, What are they not doing that I can give them? When I was a teenager writing about music, I could see no one at *The Times* was writing about youth culture, grunge, and all these important bands. So I went to them, and they saw that I could be useful. Spend an exciting hour on your laptop and write an actual list: What are the things I have to offer? If there aren't enough things on the list, you know you need to get more skills.

NEVER SAY NEVER...SAY NOT YET

You might not find the thing you love to do until you are 39, just as you might not find the guy you will love until you are 39. And then for some people, the guy moves next door when you are 20, and you think, Well, that was easy! When you have a worry, try putting the word yet at the end of it. "I haven't found what I want to do...yet." "I haven't found the guy...yet." Say "yet" and you won't feel so impatient.

NO JOB IS OFF-LIMITS

One of the things that's wrong with the education system is that you don't learn about all the jobs out there, so you tend to inherit your job from your parents' social group. You could be meant to be the world's best cage fighter, but you don't know how to get there. My education was going to the library. I read about hundreds of people with all kinds of jobs. When you read an autobiography, you become one person cleverer. You will spend more time working than you will spend sleeping, fucking, or hanging out with friends, so find something you love. If you do, you will never need Xanax.

PUT YOURSELF OUT THERE

My career started when I was 13 and I entered a contest to write about the books that I loved. So I'm all for entering competitions, and now I never say no to judging one. Judges want to love you. And if they don't? Unless by an astonishing coincidence you have the exact same name as me, I will not remember you. You've got nothing at all to lose.

YOU AREN'T WEIRD...YOUR SITUATION IS

Workplaces are geared toward straight white males. You'll have to adopt the dominant culture to an extent—it's exhausting to be iconoclastic every minute. But that culture is coming to an end. We need new ideas in government, education, the arts, business. Women, people of color, gay and trans people...they are the future, because everything else has been tried. Eventually, your difference will make you valuable.

BELIEVE IN UNICORNS

Our entire culture—the internet, reality TV, even kid shows—is snarky and sarcastic. That attitude will kill you. If you are completely comfortable with who you are, you have no need to hate other people. I want to be the one who says, "That's cool you wore that hat. It's great that you believe in that cause." You can't have big ambitions if you are a small person. Be big! Be huge! Have a big, fat, floppy optimism about the future.

Your Career Get-Ahead Guide

Three of the most important skills you need in your work toolbox are:

STEP 1

Speaking Effectively

STEP 2

Knowing How to Work With a Team

STEP 3

Learning From Your Mistakes

Want some tips on how to sharpen those skills? Read on.

1.
Speak Up–The Right Way

As **Annie Tomlin** found out, it's not only what you say at work, it's also *how* you say it. Sound more powerful, polished, and professional by tomorrow morning.

THIS WAS MY BRILLIANT Monday morning plan: Lay out the genius concepts I'd devised over the weekend and dazzle my colleagues. But I sped through my talking points, squeaked when answering tough questions, and said "totally" at least seven times. I'd hoped to make a good impression. Instead, I sounded like a helium-huffing Busta Rhymes protégée.

"To a certain degree, you are your voice," says Patricia Fletcher, a voice coach in NYC. "If your voice is free, relaxed, and expressive, it's more likely your message, ideas, and persona will be perceived the same way." And if your voice is tight, small, or constricted? "You run the risk of having your message—and you—perceived in kind." Oof. I began working with Fletcher to cultivate a powerful workplace voice.

SMOOTH IT OVER

Oh vocal fry...that gravelly, "Is she hungover?" tone you hear when Britney Spears and Emma Stone speak. It's widespread among young women, but it doesn't project clarity or confidence in the workplace. Eliminate fry and you take a huge step toward "coming across as capable, expressive, and clear," Fletcher says.

Like fryers, my voice sometimes tenses as I hold my breath between words. To replace shallow breaths with deep inhalations, I stand with a pillow on my head, which falls if I wiggle around or jut my chin forward when speaking. Then I hold my thumb in front of my mouth, extend it toward an imaginary person I'm talking to, and visualize my voice following that path.

QUIT THE BABY TALK

Logically, I know that speaking in a little-girl voice when I'm uncomfortable doesn't say badass career woman. So if my voice isn't naturally high-pitched, why do I slip into Chipette mode when I'm feeling the heat? "Women may be, consciously or subconsciously, using the same ammo that worked for them in their adolescence," Fletcher says. But while playing the innocent-and-cute card may have helped us get our way or avoid criticism as a kid, it doesn't project authority as an adult. Try yawning several times—both with your mouth open wide and pursing your lips. This stretches out your throat and tongue, which helps prevent sound from escaping through your nose—key to eliminating nasally baby voice. And if you have a naturally high-pitched voice, you can help it project more strength and confidence by spending a few minutes humming while you get ready for work each morning. "Make sure to slide around into deeper pitches to really wake up your lower register," says Fletcher.

SHUT DOWN THE UPSPEAK

You know how sometimes? Everything someone says? Rises up and sounds like a question? That's upspeak, and it conveys hesitation and confusion, Fletcher says. If your sentences end on the upswing, try this visualization exercise: as you speak, use your hand to "draw" a straight, steady line out of your mouth at the same time. My voice is more confident when I do it.

PHASE OUT THE FILLERS

Subconsciously dotting sentences with likes, ums, and ya-knows is very common...and can make people question your intelligence. The fix? Replace your likes and ums with a breath. "Take the silent second to gather your thoughts instead of filling everything with a sound," Fletcher advises. I try it and find that my colleagues no longer interrupt me. Instead, they look at me like I have something important to say. And I do.

2.
Be a Team Player

Teams don't get more major than DreamWorks Studios CEO and co-chairman **Stacey Snider** and her partner, **Steven Spielberg.** Use her tips on collaboration to charm any coworker.

READ THE VIBE OF THE ROOM.

Collaborating requires being hyper-attuned to the people around you. I recently asked Steven to read a script, and he e-mailed, "Call me when you're ready to discuss." I knew from the tone of that sentence that he didn't like it, because "I love this!" would have been an impulse he would not have resisted.

CREATE A SAFE SPACE.

I have a distinct memory of my school days. When I raised my hand or turned in a paper, there was that moment of Will I meet the test? Every time a writer turns in a script or a filmmaker shows you her film, she's utterly exposed, so I recall that feeling and try to give people the permission to share their ideas.

DON'T LEAP TO SAY NO.

When someone pitches an idea, I try to withhold immediate judgment. You can pause for at least a few seconds, consider what's been said, and be thoughtful when you respond. If a director said, "I think we should turn this intense drama into a musical," I might say, "We should think about that overnight." Sometimes I take the time to process the idea, even if it is just a tactic!

What are you known for as a boss? Empathic management: I try to build collegiality and common purpose.	**What do you wear to work?** I always want to buy flashy statement pieces, but I end up with well-tailored black trousers and jackets and blouses. It is chic and saves me from wasting a ton of money.	**How do you keep from overworking?** Discipline. You say you're going to leave at a certain time, you stand up, and you go home. Do it a while and it becomes easier.	**Your favorite advice?** Your career is a long-term project. You will put your foot on the gas or on the brake at different times, but try not to stop entirely.

SAY "WE," NOT "I."

Sometimes I want to say, "Are you crazy? That's a terrible idea!" But instead, I say, "I'm not sure we should go down this path." What could be more namby-pamby than that sentence? I'm then able to follow it with "Instead, I think we should do this," and 9 out of 10 times, they agree. I'm not able to say the second sentence without the first.

SHARE THE CREDIT.

I don't deny my own achievements, but when I get a congratulatory e-mail about a film, I respond, "Thank you for your kind words. I hope you recommend the film because your opinions matter." I consider my ability to share credit a measure of my own status. You're more powerful if you can afford to be generous.

DON'T EXPECT TO LIKE EVERYONE.

You will have collaborators you just don't click with, and you'll develop a bag of tricks. If it's someone who's shy, you may have to ask leading questions to draw him or her out. If it's someone you find distasteful, you can affect a friendly attitude. Why invest too much emotionally? Your goal is to finish the project or sign someone to the deal. It isn't to be their best friend.

3.

Learn From Your Screw-Ups

Even when you work for a runaway success, things will go wrong, says **Emily White**, 35, a veteran of Google, Facebook, Instagram, and most recently, Snapchat. So make your worst days work for you.

BOUNCE BACK FROM THE LITTLE MISTAKES

EXPECT TO BE WRONG

When I was weighing leaving a job that I loved to work with Snapchat, my husband told me, "People who don't take risks work for people who do." Which is so true! And you can't take risks and avoid mistakes. That is completely incongruent. Our education system tends to train kids to be right rather than to learn. But as long as you're learning, I don't care if you're wrong. It means you are trying new things.

OWN UP QUICKLY

Solving a problem is great, but don't let that mean you sit around for a week or two before you surface it. I love team members who say, "Just so you know, no one was looking and I messed up." I then trust that person more. They just proved to me that they have the radar to understand when they messed up and that they're optimizing for the company and not for themselves.

SEIZE THE MOMENT

Realize that when you mess up, you just got insight on how to help yourself in the future. It's a gift. So many people miss that opportunity to learn. You're busy, and you hope so badly that you could just return to normal. The really clever people are able not only to return to a baseline but also to make it better. Have the presence of mind to ask, "How do I turn this into an advantage?"

BUT DON'T DWELL ON IT

Companies that do well are incredibly focused—they know where they want to pay attention and what's a distraction. At Snapchat, we want it to be all about the product, so we've hired mostly engineers. And it's the same with where you put your own energy. If I beat myself up about not responding to an e-mail, that is going to take up my headspace and prevent me from spending energy on bigger questions.

AVOID THE BIG MISTAKES

PICK THE RIGHT COMPANY

If you're with a bad company, you're not going anywhere. If a company is moving in the right direction, you can do good things and move yourself into other roles over time.

DON'T JUST FOLLOW ORDERS

Especially right out of school, we do what other people ask without questioning it. At Facebook, I was hired to build a local-deals business. I spent a year on it before I asked, "Is this actually right for us?" I had to dismantle what I'd built. If I'm the leader I was meant to be, it was my responsibility to redirect things earlier on.

ALWAYS ASK "WHY?"

If I see someone doing something I think is wrong, I ask, "Why did you make that decision?" People want to share their thinking, and talking it through often leads to a better solution for the company.

The Field Guide to Working With MEN

THERE IS NO "I" IN SUCCESS. Nor is there in power, a fatter paycheck, and promotion—oops, yes, there's an "I" in that. The point is, getting ahead in your career doesn't happen in a vacuum. You won't climb very far without a professional support network, which should include work friends who have your back, a boss who recognizes your value, and a mentor who keeps you on track. Assembling the dream team is a challenge—and it can be doubly so when many of your coworkers, managers, and maybe mentors are men, who not only tend to have different ways of collaborating and communicating than you do but who also tend to set the tone in the workplace.

Women today are starting their careers better-educated than their male

To get to the top, you need support from coworkers and superiors—namely those with chest hair. Do it while being the fabulous woman you are.

peers and making more money relative to men their age than their mothers did, according to Pew Research—but company culture starts from the top, and the top is still teeming with testosterone. "The global average of women in senior management is only 20 percent," says Barbara Annis, founding partner of Gender Intelligence Group, a consulting firm. "Leaders are slowly coming around to cracking the code on that. Research shows that companies perform better financially when more women are in high-level positions."

The key word: slowly. You are not delusional for wondering if you've ever been dismissed or unfairly perceived simply for carrying two X chromosomes. "It can take young women years to realize that experiences they've had in the workplace are gender-related," says Melissa Thomas-Hunt, PhD, associate professor of business administration at the University of Virginia, who studies gender and racial bias in the workplace. "Men and women have interacted since childhood, but the familiarity is deceptive. In the workforce, there are organizational norms that favor men and disadvantage women."

Our workplaces have work to do to support women. But in the meantime, you have names to take and dragons to slay. While you should never change who you are because of workplace sexism, you do need skills—whether it's avoiding miscommunication or benefiting from a male mentor without everyone thinking you're sleeping with him. Play it right and men will help launch you to the top.

WHEN YOU WANT A MENTOR

Who wouldn't? But it's a tricky business. Use these strategies to navigate the minefield that is the opposite-sex mentorship.

LAND MINE

Your options are men who only mentor other men.

DODGE IT: "You can earn the trust of a male superior," says Sylvia Ann Hewlett, PhD, founder and CEO of the Center for Talent Innovation. To attract a sponsor, she says, understand that it's not all about you. Your job is to deliver results and display a great work ethic so, in turn, your sponsor can pass golden opportunities your way.

He's very busy and very intimidating.

DODGE IT: Asking someone point-blank to sponsor you rarely works. He doesn't care why you want him to mentor you...but he probably would like sharing advice on something he knows. Go in prepared. Maybe note that he has a large client list and say you would love suggestions on how to grow your own.

He's afraid of coming across like he's hitting on you.

DODGE IT: "Men aren't sure what the right protocol is around a woman and will err on the side of caution when it comes to approaching you," says Annis. Grow the relationship by asking him to coffee or lunch. Tell him that you value the advice he's given you so far and you would love to continue your career talks.

LAND MINE

The whole office thinks you're sleeping with him.

DODGE IT: "Tell coworkers, 'Bill has been mentoring me, and he's been really supportive,'" suggests Kim Elsesser, PhD, research scholar at the Center for the Study of Women at UCLA and author of *Sex and the Office*. Keep doors open, and hang out in the cafeteria. Then if anyone spots you socializing outside the office, nothing seems amiss.

Mentorships are tricky for women at your company.

DODGE IT: "By assigning men to mentor women, your company can encourage male-female mentorships and create a new norm where men aren't hesitant to support women," says Annis. Tell your human resources department that you've read about other mentorship program successes and you're game to try.

"When I first got signed...
I thought my whole world
was going to turn around.
I thought I was going to
be on *Oprah* the next
week....I was lucky enough
to have someone like Jay
saying: 'This isn't good
enough. You have
to find yourself.'"

—RITA ORA, WHO IS WITH
JAY Z'S ROC NATION LABEL

"[Roland Mouret] helped
me put a very small team
together that would help
turn my dreams and my
designs into a reality."

—VICTORIA BECKHAM

"[*The Office* creator]
Greg Daniels has been key
to just about everything
I've done these past eight
years. He's the best."

—MINDY KALING

"If Ralph [Lauren] believed in you, he really believed in you. And he really supported and believed in me." —VERA WANG

"He's incredibly trusting, so that's very empowering to an individual. That trust makes me not want to disappoint Warren [Buffett], Berkshire, or shareholders."
—TRACY BRITT COOL, CEO, PAMPERED CHEF, AND FORMER FINANCIAL ASSISTANT TO BUFFETT AT BERKSHIRE HATHAWAY

"During my years [at *SNL*], my relationship with Lorne [Michaels] transitioned from terrified pupil and reluctant teacher to small-town girl and streetwise madam showing her the ropes to Annie and Daddy Warbucks...to a bond of mutual respect and friendship." —TINA FEY

Does He Get What You're Saying?

Miscommunication can lead to conflict, especially between men and women. We explain how to prevent your wires from getting crossed.

1

HE THINKS
She just told me what a great job *my team* did on the sales presentation—uh, what about me?

YOU'RE PRETTY SURE
I just gave Mike a really nice compliment—maybe we'll become friends now!

COMPROMISE
A large amount of testosterone is released when a man gets individual acknowledgment. If you think he's done well, praise him and he'll thank you.

2

HE THINKS
She's agreed with me because she was nodding her head and murmuring "Mmm-hmmm" the whole time.

YOU'RE PRETTY SURE
Um, that's just how I listen, and I think that's a terrible idea, actually.

COMPROMISE
Women tend to engage in "active listening" (nodding while someone else speaks). Men take this to mean you're on the same page. If you're not, be cognizant of this behavior.

3

HE THINKS
She's not very
confident about that
idea or suggestion
she voiced in
a meeting.

**YOU'RE
PRETTY SURE**
I'm sharing a
staggeringly brilliant idea
with you. Bow down.

COMPROMISE
Instead of asking,
"What do you think?" start singing
your own praises: "I've really
thought this through; this is a great
idea. Hear me out."

4

HE THINKS
Women ask too many
questions in meetings,
and it slows
everything down.

**YOU'RE
PRETTY SURE**
Asking questions shows your
interest and commitment
to a project and is one of your
greatest contributions.

COMPROMISE
Declare your intentions up front.
Say, "My goal is to be sure we're
absolutely analytical in this situation, so I'm going to ask a few
questions."

SOURCE: BARBARA ANNIS, GENDER
INTELLIGENCE GROUP   **73**

THE 10 COMMANDMENTS
for dating a coworker

Sometimes, you fall in love on the job. Just write these rules in stone
before (and after) you hook up.

1

Thou shall first get the lowdown on the company interoffice-dating policy. Forbidden? Keep it in thy pants.

2

Have the hots for thy coworker? Thou shall keep it discreet until you know it's reciprocated.

3

Thou shall treat office dating like ice cream: Indulge sparingly…and the object of your affection better be Talenti.

4

If someone asks, thou shall come clean. Don't give anyone a reason to think you're not trustworthy.

5

Ready to "come out"? Thou shall tell thy boss first, then thy coworkers.

6

Thou shall treat each other professionally and never, ever give thy lover preferential treatment.

7

Thou shall not post cutesy, incriminating pics you wouldn't want coworkers to see on Instagram or Facebook.

8

Thou shall continue to foster relationships and friendships by socializing with other coworkers.

9

Thou shall not fight, engage in baby talk, or use thy work computer to send naughty e-mails while on the clock.

10

Thou shall not bad-mouth him at work if you break up. Even if he cheated. Even if he cheated with thy sister.

Keep Him in the Friend Zone

Why did the Mayans go extinct? How could Amy Poehler and Will Arnett break up? Can men and women be friends? We can now answer one of these eternal questions: While you can have opposite-sex friends, the same can't always be said for him.

"Men tend to misperceive friendliness as sexual or romantic interest," says Kim Elsesser, PhD. In a 2012 study in the *Journal of Social and Personal Relationships*, men were more likely to report an attraction to their platonic female friends than vice versa and to assume that those romantic feelings were mutual, a woefully misguided belief.

Send the message that you're not interested at the outset. If you have a partner, introduce him around the office.

If you still get a flirty vibe, say: "I'm sure you're joking around, but it makes me uncomfortable." (That gives him an easy out to say, "Oh yeah, I was just kidding.") If the direct approach fails, try the "third grade" method: Have a trusted colleague pass the message. If needed, head to your manager or HR. "You have every right to feel safe and comfortable at work," Elsesser says.

Is it gross that women must know how to fend off a coworker's sexual advances in 2015? Yes. But is it reality? Same answer, unfortunately.

CRACK THE DUDE CODE

Here's a playbook on how to bond with him effectively and authentically.

Sports Talk

I'm not into it.

It's fine if you think March Madness is caused by long winters. Study up a little with sporty friends, if you want, and look for ways to steer work convos to neutral turf.

I'm an armchair commentator.

"Sports talk tends to become competition for men," says Elsesser. Weigh in on LeBron vs. MJ, but know that the debate may not net you friendship.

Recreational Fun

I wasn't invited (rude).

Inject yourself into social outings and it will start to feel like the norm. When the guys are going out without you, say, "Sounds great! What time?"

I was invited, but *meh*.

You mean you don't like to spend all your downtime smoking cigars? Take the reins and plan gender-neutral activities, like a 5K race or a dinner, suggests Elsesser.

TV Shows

I'm a loyal viewer.

"Take note of the topics that bring your male coworkers together," says Elsesser. Have strong opinions on Don Draper too? Get in there.

I'm a total cord cutter.

"All coworkers have their work in common," says Elsesser. Giving people helpful tips on coworkers can increase bonds, so go tell Jim that Tina will like his ideas better after her a.m. coffee.

26 Way$
to Have More
Money Now

Cosmo financial columnist and LearnVest founder
Alexa von Tobel shares some painless ways to earn more,
save more, and spend less this year.
(Don't panic—you don't have to give up your morning latte.)

1 Start a $5 jar. Loose change adds up. Want it to add up faster? Anytime you have a fiver in your wallet, jar it. You'll have $50 before you know it.

2 Unplug devices...Ten percent of each electricity bill is for stuff that you don't even have turned on! Unplug gadgets and see your bill shrink.

3 ...or sell them off. Have random old electronics collecting dust? Gazelle.com will buy smartphones, tablets, and more. An iPhone 4 could get you more than $100.

4 Plan your shopping. Making daily trips to the grocery store seems practical, but studies show you'll spend at least 50 percent more than you want/expect to. Take one well-planned trip to the market each week.

5 Bundle your services. A package that includes cable, internet, and phone tends to be cheaper than one for only cable or internet—even if you have no intention of using your home phone.

6 Cut back on cable. Speaking of cable, the average U.S. subscriber spends $900 per year. Spend less by switching it off during vacations, accessing content for less on HuluPlus or Netflix, or using an Apple TV or Chromecast device to stream your favorite shows à la carte.

7 Unload extra tickets. Can't make the concert or the big game? A new site, LyteUp.com, will quote you a price on your seats within 30 minutes and zap the funds directly to your bank account. Way less hassle than Craigslist or eBay.

8 Customize your phone. If you tend to go over your allotted minutes, texts, or data, you could save $50 a month with a customized plan. And choose Wi-Fi over 4G whenever possible—it will lower your data usage.

9 Get paid to shop. Download the free EasyShift app, and use it while you're running errands to do tasks for retailers' research departments, like seeing if a product is in stock. You score $2 to $4 per task.

10 Don't spend on H_2O. Buy bottled water twice a week and in three months, you'll have dropped $50. Tap water is equally healthy—and free.

11 Book ahead. At OpenTable.com, restaurant reservations earn you cash for dinners out. As few as five bookings could add up to a $50 credit.

12 Turn up the fridge. Raise your fridge and freezer temp by five degrees and save about $50 each year (but keep it below 40 degrees to keep food fresh).

13 Skip ATM fees. At up to $3 per transaction, speedy cash could easily cost you $50 this year...or month. The free Allpoint app helps you find surcharge-free ATMs near your current locale.

14 Be an errand girl. At TaskRabbit.com, you can get paid to do chores for others. Fifty bucks to put together an Ikea dresser: Why not?

15 Max out your savings. Transfer your money from a checking account to a high-yield savings account. With rates online close to 1 percent annual percentage yield, you can earn $10 for every $1,000 you deposit. It feels great to have your bank pay you for once.

16 Sign up for a commuter-reimbursement account if your employer offers one. You can avoid taxes on some of your getting-to-work costs (parking, gas, subway fare), saving you hundreds of dollars per year.

17 Check out Savored.com, which discounts your meal based on what time of day you reserve—eating at geezer o'clock could save you 40 percent.

18 Use the Happy Hours app to find drink deals (free, iTunes.com and Google.Play.com).

19 Seek out adventures that don't cost you anything: gratis concerts, museum free days, farmers' markets, or beach or trail hikes. It's a scientific fact that experiences bring you more happiness than stuff does.

20 Always negotiate your rent—even in a competitive market. PadMapper.com finds vacancies and the median price for similar rentals.

21 Sidestep brokers' fees by finding no-fee apartments on Apartable.com.

22 Do a quick energy audit. Is your air conditioner on a timer? Lights off? Cords plugged into power strips so you can turn everything off with one switch? Plugged-in electronics suck energy even if they're not in use—costing an estimated $200 per year per household.

23 Pay credit-card bills twice a month. Interest compounds daily, so making an extra payment reduces what you owe, whether or not you carry a balance.

24 Ditch overdraft protection. It comes with fees and encourages overspending.

25 Separate your savings and checking accounts. Savings in a checking account tend to get spent.

26 Take a money-management class. The ones at LearnVest.com/Classes can help you set up a budget, grasp investing basics, max out your 401(k), and a lot more.

Your Sleep

Jump-start your baller status by investing what you have and making your money work—even when you're not.

—Alexa von Tobel

INVESTING. Let me guess: You think it's something you should be doing but have no idea where to start? Join the club! According to a survey by Wells Fargo, 71 percent of women feel like they are not knowledgeable enough to invest in today's market. If you break through the fear and invest your money, it can grow without your even touching it.

THAT'S BECAUSE COMPOUND INTEREST IS A MAGICAL THING.

Let's say you start with $365 that earns 5 percent interest per year. Look what happens next:

YEAR 1	YEAR 5	YEAR 10
$365	**$465.50**	**$1577.51**

Here's How It Works

When you're ready to invest your money, you can open an investment account at…

1. A bank
2. A full-service brokerage
3. A mutual fund company
4. A discount brokerage

WHY? You'll generally pay lower fees with a discount brokerage and, therefore, have more money to invest. You, the investor, are charged a fee to buy and sell stocks and bonds, but you don't get the white-glove (more expensive) treatment like you would at a traditional brokerage. Some discount brokerages offer an initial bonus for opening an account.

START

Before-You-Begin Checklist

1 Tackle your credit-card debt. With interest rates averaging 15 percent, this should be a high priority.

2 Set up an emergency fund with at least six months of net income. You May Now Pass Go!

PICK YOUR

#WealthGoals

Decide what you want your money to do. Do you want to save for your first apartment? Do you want to buy a small island someday? Do you want to retire when you're 50 instead of when you're 70? How you invest may depend on what your goals are.

FIVE-YEAR PLAN

Consider investing money that you won't need for at least five years. Investing money to build your dream home in 10 years? Probably smart. Investing money for next summer's vacation? Probably risky.

JUMP IN

Most people start investing through a retirement plan.

401(k): Invests money from your pre-tax paycheck. Employers often match employee contributions.

IRA: Individual retirement account that has tax advantages. You open this account yourself, which is when you'd look for a brokerage.

NOW WHAT?

What does your portfolio look like?
Because the stock market is always changing, your portfolio's original mix of stocks and bonds will likely shift over time. Think about investing for retirement or other goals over a long-time horizon and don't overreact to small ups and downs.

Set up an annual credit alert.
Check that your portfolio is still balanced, meaning it has a range of fund types appropriate for the level of risk you want to handle.

What to check for when you're shopping around for a brokerage:

ACCOUNT MINIMUMS.
How much is required to start?
COMMISSIONS.
How much do they charge for trades?
MANAGEMENT FEES.
Are there any ongoing fees?
SERVICES.
What do they offer to help you?
WEBSITE.
Do you like using the site? Is it intuitive and easy to use?

FINISH

CAUTION!

Opening an account is good, but your retirement contribution might not be invested until you select funds. Don't let your money waste away in cash reserves. (This probably won't be the case with a 401(k), which usually defaults to an investment option if you don't actively select one yourself.)

SET YOUR MONEY ON ITS COURSE

Research your investing options. Different funds do different things. Aim for low-fee options like exchange-traded funds, or ETFs. Try not to get caught up in the confusing names of funds. Many brokerages offer a basic risk-tolerance quiz. That can be a great starting point.

INVESTING CAN BE TRICKY.
So ask for help! Consider consulting a professional, such as a registered investment adviser (RIA).

How to Get More Money When...

YOU'RE
APPLYING
FOR A
NEW
JOB

Asking for more money isn't comfortable. But research shows that 66 percent of the time, women who request a higher salary get it. Negotiation expert **Kim Keating**, founder and CEO of the Keating Advisors consulting firm, is with you at each step.

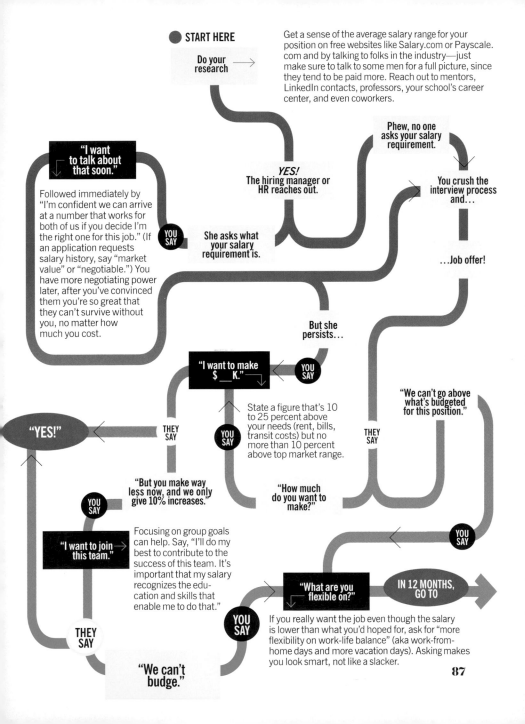

START HERE

Do your research →

Get a sense of the average salary range for your position on free websites like Salary.com or Payscale.com and by talking to folks in the industry—just make sure to talk to some men for a full picture, since they tend to be paid more. Reach out to mentors, LinkedIn contacts, professors, your school's career center, and even coworkers.

"I want to talk about that soon."

Followed immediately by "I'm confident we can arrive at a number that works for both of us if you decide I'm the right one for this job." (If an application requests salary history, say "market value" or "negotiable.") You have more negotiating power later, after you've convinced them you're so great that they can't survive without you, no matter how much you cost.

YES! The hiring manager or HR reaches out.

YOU SAY

She asks what your salary requirement is.

Phew, no one asks your salary requirement.

You crush the interview process and...

...Job offer!

But she persists...

YOU SAY

"I want to make $___K."

State a figure that's 10 to 25 percent above your needs (rent, bills, transit costs) but no more than 10 percent above top market range.

YOU SAY

"We can't go above what's budgeted for this position."

THEY SAY

"YES!"

THEY SAY

"But you make way less now, and we only give 10% increases."

YOU SAY

"How much do you want to make?"

YOU SAY

"I want to join this team."

Focusing on group goals can help. Say, "I'll do my best to contribute to the success of this team. It's important that my salary recognizes the education and skills that enable me to do that."

"What are you flexible on?"

IN 12 MONTHS, GO TO

YOU SAY

If you really want the job even though the salary is lower than what you'd hoped for, ask for "more flexibility on work-life balance" (aka work-from-home days and more vacation days). Asking makes you look smart, not like a slacker.

THEY SAY

"We can't budge."

87

How to Get More Money When...

YOU WANT A RAISE AT YOUR
CURRENT JOB

● **START HERE**

Keep a log.

It's easy to forget all your tiny and T. Rex successes as the days blur together—write them down so they're at the top of your mind when you're ready to ask for a raise.

Lay the groundwork.

Your boss can't possibly know the extent of your successes and contributions. Find creative ways to fill her in. Example: Pop by her office to talk about a success, then ask her opinion on your next step. This gets her up to speed on your awesomeness and makes a raise convo feel less awkward and out of nowhere.

Do any of these scenarios describe your current state?

● It's at least 90 days before your performance evaluation. Budgets often get locked in a quarter before review season, so now is the time to say you want a raise.

● You just took on a new responsibility. Your manager thinks you can handle the big stuff, making it a great time to ask for a bigger paycheck.

● You just inherited someone else's workload. Whether it was staff layoffs or something else, if your workload has grown, so should your salary.

Hold off a bit.

Waiting until you've been in your position for at least 12 months gives you a performance history to use as leverage for a raise.

Have you been there a year?

YES   NO

"YES!"

She agrees to bump you up! Aren't you glad you asked?

THEY SAY

There's never been a better time to ask for more money.

Figure out what title and salary you're going to request. Your goal: a 10 percent bump.

YOU SAY

NO   YES

You should still ask for a raise.

But keep it in the 4-percent-more-than-you-make-now neighborhood.

YOU SAY

"Could we meet about me?"

No boss wants to be blindsided. Plus, giving her a heads-up means she has time to try to secure more funds for you. E-mail your boss this: "I'd love to talk about my performance and future. Do you have a few minutes so we can meet?"

THEY SAY

"Let's meet on Monday."

"What a great year..."

Kick off the conversation by focusing on the company. Say, "It's been a great year for the team, and I've learned so much. I want to talk with you about my career and my compensation." Be specific about your goals: "I feel my performance has earned me [the title you want] and compensation [the salary you want]." Point out your successes.

YOU SAY

"I still love my job."

Be positive: Say how much you love collaborating with the team, then ask for suggestions on positioning yourself for a raise in the future. End with this: "Can I circle back in six months to revisit?" Now you're in a great spot as new resources and positions open up.

YOU SAY

"No one is getting a raise this year." "You're not ready."

THEY SAY

89

PARTY!
It's Good for Your Career

Mika Brzezinski, Cosmo columnist and *Morning Joe* cohost, knows how to work the room. Follow her lead to supercharge your work and social life.

5 P.M.

MAYBE I SHOULD SKIP IT... Why rally to work-related cocktail parties, networking events, and luncheons? Because you're going to make them work for you. And it's fun! If your work connects you with people you enjoy and respect, your career will be better for it. So don't go in thinking, I have to be the life of the party, because if people like me, they'll hire me. Think, Connecting with people I share interests with is fun. I recently met Sallie Krawcheck, whose Pax Ellevate Global Women's Index Fund invests in companies that advance women. We're both so passionate about this issue that I predict we'll be good friends. If you like how someone works, you'll like them too.

6 P.M.

UGH, I DON'T KNOW A SOUL. You make more connections when you go it alone, because you're forced to be social. Find out the purpose of the event, who's running it, and the name of someone you want to meet there. Once there, introduce yourself to the host and chat about the event's mission. Then mention anyone you want to meet, and say you're a big admirer and wanted to say it in person. Making intros helps people feel important, so they're usually happy to do it when they can. (I've even seen a few marriages happen this way!)

7 P.M.

HMM, WHAT TO SAY NEXT...

When you are chatting with someone, ask a question and let her talk. Shut up and listen. Don't be afraid of a moment of silence—it's worse if you say something dumb because you're so eager to be entertaining. When you feel like you've gotten everything you can out of the encounter, look the person in the eye, shake her hand, and say it was great to meet her. If you must, say you need to find the host to thank her, but as long as you're polite, don't worry about escaping—it's always a good idea to leave them wanting more.

8 P.M.

THAT WAS ACTUALLY FUN.

What now? If there's someone you want to know better, e-mail her on the night of the event, while you're still fresh in her mind. But make it count....Don't just do a "nice to meet you." Move the engagement forward—whether it's business or personal that you have in mind, you should give her a genuine compliment or set up another meeting. My business partnership with Arianna Huffington happened because she e-mailed and asked me to breakfast after we chatted at a party. Nobody is better at follow-up than she is, and our breakfast conversation turned into our Thrive conference series!

REMEMBER YOUR PHONE, for taking down people's info... or selfies with new friends. Forget standing alone, hunched, and texting. That says "Please don't talk to me."

REMEMBER: TAKE PEOPLE'S BUSINESS CARD OR CONTACT INFO. Forget waiting for them to e-mail you. Work it!

REMEMBER: WEAR AMAZING SHOES. They start conversations. Forget any shoes you can't walk in. Wobbling does not look powerful.

Stand Out the Right Way

Everyone wants to be noticed...but not for the wrong reasons. Mika flags a few easy-to-make mistakes, and how to avoid them.

CRASHING THE CONVERSATION

The two people in the cubicle next to you are very quietly working through an issue—doesn't matter if it's personal or work-related—and you are sure you know the answer to their problem. Resist the urge to jump in just because you can hear them. They didn't ask for your help saving the day, and there's a good chance they'll be annoyed that you interrupted their private conversation.

GOING OFF AT WORK

It's a wonderful thing to enjoy your work and to do it exuberantly. But let your work and upbeat attitude shine instead of acting out in distracting ways. Laugh at jokes, but not so loudly that people turn their heads. Whispering with coworkers can make your colleagues nervous ("are they talking about me?"). And don't be such a loud talker that you distract your cubemates—if you aren't sure, just ask them.

RANDOMLY BRAGGING

You should absolutely raise your hand when you have something to add. But don't feel you need to prove yourself in every conversation. When your boss kicks off Monday morning's meeting with "I hope everyone had a good weekend...," you can smile genuinely and nod, instead of launching into the story about how you scored the new iPhone 6, sat front row at the Nicki Minaj concert, or chatted up a big name in your field at a party. If you drop names or waste people's time, they'll be annoyed, not impressed.

OBSESSING OVER YOUR NEXT MOVE

When interacting with your manager, try not to talk excessively about all the big stuff you want to take on soon or the next job you want at the company. That puts down the job you already have. When I was at CBS, the president of the network told me that he was so refreshed to hear how much I loved my job that it made him want to see me doing more because I showed such spirit and joy.

SHOWING UP LATE

We're all busy, but don't wear your frazzled-ness on your sleeve. Plan your calendar so you can be at every dinner, lunch, meeting, coffee, and conference call three minutes early. I learned this years ago at a luncheon with some of the most important and influential women in Manhattan. There was a mistake with my schedule, and I ended up arriving halfway through the lunch. I was mortified I'd kept these busy women waiting—and I will never make that mistake again.

"I'm Not Ashamed of Getting Fired"

WHEN JILL ABRAMSON WAS APPOINTED the first female executive editor of *The New York Times*, it was a big deal. When she was fired only two and a half years into the gig for her "brusque management style," it was an even bigger deal, making headlines across the globe. She gave Cosmo an exclusive first interview after it happened, where she talked about how to get ahead...and fight your way back.

BOXING GLOVES I knew I was being fired beforehand, but it went public on a Wednesday. My kids were upset, and the loudness of the coverage was surprising. So I arrived at my trainer's in Manhattan, where I always went early on Thursdays. He had these boxing gloves, and he said, "You need this." I said, "Take a picture of me." I wanted to send it to my kids to see I wasn't at home crying and sitting in a corner. Within a nanosecond, my daughter, Cornelia, had put it on Instagram, and it went viral. The next morning, it was on the cover of the *New York Post*. I did the boxing once more after that. It felt fantastic.

MEN VS. WOMEN What [*New York Times* publisher] Arthur Sulzberger Jr. has said publicly is that he had problems with my management style. The whole issue of how women's management styles are viewed is an incredibly interesting subject. In some ways, the reaction was much bigger when Politico ran this hatchet job on me [the profile by Dylan Byers called her "stubborn," "condescending," and "uncaring"]. If there is a silver lining, it was the giant reaction from other women journalists. These women editors at the *Chicago Tribune*, who I have never met, sent me flowers after that article.

NO SHAME Is it hard to say I was fired? No. I've said it about 20 times, and it's not. I was in fact insistent that that be publicly clear because I was not ashamed of that. And I don't think young women—it's hard, I know—should feel stigmatized if they are fired. Especially in this economy, people are fired right and left for arbitrary reasons, and there are sometimes forces beyond your control.

TEARS I think it is important to try to speak very candidly to young women. The most important advice I would still give—and it may seem crazy because I did lose this job I really loved—is you have to be an authentic person. I did cry. That is my authentic first reaction. I don't regret sharing that.

CHEER SQUAD It helps that my husband and I have been together since sophomore year at Harvard. Having him in my corner and my kids and my sister helps. My sister called me up after I got fired to say our father would be as proud of me that morning as when I got the job. That's sort of how you dust yourself off.

HER POSSE This is going to sound incredibly out of it, but I didn't read in real time what was written about me and losing my job. It was a survival mechanism. A lot of my friends [like Maureen Dowd, Michiko Kakutani, Jane Mayer, Ellen Pollock] were like my medieval food tasters. They read, and if I really needed to know something, they would tell me. One thing I love is TheLi.st, an e-mail group of women in their 20s and 30s. I was a very big thread. TheLi.sters called me a badass, which is a cool thing in their view. And I'm like, "I am!" But, you know, it's a little dangerous to be a badass.

REJECTION The times I didn't get jobs I wanted, I remember feeling dispirited, really crestfallen. I didn't get a job as [then Secretary of State] Cyrus Vance's speech writer in 1977 or 1978. But be careful what you wish for. It can be best to get passed over for a job, as there may be a better job out there. After that, I was hired into the election unit of NBC News.

SEXISM AT WORK Of course I experienced sexism early on. I remember being in story sessions, and so many times, I would have an idea and I would talk about it. Then the convener of the meeting would say, "And as Jerry was just saying..." and they would remember the idea as coming from a male colleague. I didn't pipe up in real time. I did grouse about it with other women in the office, which in some ways is safer and more cowardly but is very comforting and kind of gratifying.

PAYDAYS My advice on getting a raise is what everybody's advice is: to become a confident negotiator, but that is so hard. My admiration for women who are good at that is unbridled. Women in general have a harder time talking about money with their bosses. It's part of that syndrome, like you're so lucky just to have the job. Sheryl Sandberg has written very brilliantly about this in *Lean In* and in her TED talk. Men never chalk up their success to luck but women often do. In my experience, men more often than women brought up money and talked about it and pressed for what they wanted in terms of salary before they agreed to be promoted.

POINT OF PRIDE When I was managing editor, for the first time the masthead [the list of top editors at the *Times*] was half women, but it was because they were great and they deserved it. I am totally proud of that.

NETWORKING TIP A lot of younger staffers just asked me to coffee. There's a way to do networking that isn't overly brown-nosing. I was fine if someone just said, "I want to have coffee and talk about my career."

BEYOND WORK It can be a danger to define yourself by your job. I miss my colleagues and the substance of my work, but I don't miss saying "Jill Abramson, executive editor." I don't. I was once told that a former executive editor of the *Times*, who knew he was going to stop being editor, made sure to make reservations at a particular restaurant because he was afraid after that they wouldn't give him a table anymore. That's not high on my priority list!

FOR JOURNOS I taught at Yale for five years when I was managing editor, and what I tried to stress for students interested in journalism, rather than picking a specialty, like blogging or being a videographer, was to master the basics of really good storytelling, have curiosity and a sense of how a topic is different from a story, and actually go out and witness and report. If you hone those skills, you will be in demand, as those talents are prized. There is too much journalism right now that is just based on people scraping the Internet and riffing off something else.

THE NEXT PRESIDENT? I met Hillary Clinton for the first time in 1978. I was writing for a political consulting firm, and Bill was running for governor and was one of the firm's clients. I went to Little Rock for two weeks to gather material. I was impressed that Bill Clinton had this very smart lawyer wife and this very brash woman as his top political lieutenant, Betsey Wright. Later, I went to work at American Lawyer, and I relied on Hillary as a source. Anytime I was calling her for her own expertise, she was fantastic, friendly, and helpful. But as First Lady and as a candidate's wife, she was sometimes angry at me and at some of the stories I wrote. Both [Bill and Hillary] have first-class minds, and that is a great building block for a successful presidency.

LEISURE TIME I now have time to read the whole *New York Times* print paper literally every day. It's great, I love it. I love the institution still.

WHAT'S NEXT I still love to write and report, and I'm doing some writing. A lot of news organizations have approached me. I know I don't really want to run something again right now.

ABRAMSON IN THE *TIMES* NEWSROOM IN 2013, WHEN THE *TIMES* WON FOUR PULITZER PRIZES.

Can You Be a Sexy Feminist?

Hating the F word is easy. Defining it for yourself is the tricky—but most rewarding—part. **Roxane Gay** explains.

PEOPLE HAVE SHUNNED the feminist label almost from the minute the movement began. And you know? I totally get it. When I was younger, I disavowed feminism with alarming frequency. When I was called a feminist, it felt like an insult. In fact, it was usually intended as such. What I heard was "You are an angry, sex- and man-hating victim lady person."

So I, too, boldly stated that I wasn't a feminist. I was convinced that to be a feminist, I couldn't enjoy the things that I enjoy. Now I know better. As a human, I have imperfect desires—which makes me an imperfect or a bad feminist, if you will.

For starters, I dance my ass off to songs that say terrible things about women. Let's be clear: I get angry about offensive lyrics. Still, I have to dance because the beat is so damn hot. I am currently single, but I am not a nun and I have no problem falling to my knees in, shall we say, moments of appreciation. Pink is my favorite color, and while I don't wear stilettos, I enjoy window-shopping for them.

I also enjoy when a man holds a door open for me. I believe all things yard, trash removal, and vehicle maintenance are man work. And killing spiders is never on my agenda.

Still, I hold certain truths to be self-evident. Women are equal to men. We deserve to be paid the same as a man for equal work. We have the right to dress and move through the world as we please, free from gross catcalling or the threat of violence. We have the right to easy, affordable access to birth control and reproductive services. We have the right to make choices about our bodies free from legislative oversight. And we have the right to earn respect. While I am not well-versed in feminist history and I have interests and opinions that may not fall in line with mainstream feminism, I am still a feminist. I cannot tell you how freeing it's been to accept this about myself.

In my teens and 20s, I worried that feminism wouldn't allow me to be the mess of a woman I knew myself to be. All too often, we act as if there is a right and wrong way to be a feminist, when that's not the case. We can and should adopt the kind of feminism that best suits who we are and what we want. If getting political isn't your thing, that's fine. There is no one true essential feminism that dictates how you have to be. Your own brand of feminism is what you make it...and can be as simple as a hashtag (#YesAllWomen, #SorryNotSorry).

Bottom line: Feminism is grounded in supporting the choices of women even if we wouldn't make certain choices for ourselves.

Whatever feminism you choose—good, bad, flawed, or half-assed—the label isn't something to fear. It doesn't mean you want too much or despise men. It means you believe in the equality and rights of everyone—and there's absolutely no shame in that game.

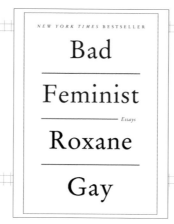

NEW YORK TIMES BESTSELLER

Bad

Feminist

Essays

Roxane

Gay

Roxane Gay is a columnist for Salon and author of *An Untamed State*. Her book, *Bad Feminist*, published by Harper Perennial, is available wherever books are sold.

MEN ON FEMINISM

We asked some of our favorite guys to read **Sheryl Sandberg**'s
Lean In and tell us what resonated most with them. Read on…

"The book brings up a good point that we should label women by their achievements, not their gender. When I think of Jodie Gatt, my COO, she is also my best friend. I don't introduce her as the woman COO of my company—it's just COO. Just as it's important to support women and men in the workforce, it's important to support them if they choose to be at home. We should support everyone's choices and continue to work on eliminating all gender bias."

—CURTIS STONE, CHEF/OWNER OF MAUDE IN BEVERLY HILLS

"I full-heartedly agree when Ms. Sandberg says that the key is to sit at the table. If you've earned a seat at the table, then sit at the table and own it!"

—VICTOR CRUZ, WIDE RECEIVER FOR THE NEW YORK GIANTS

"This book, particularly for male leaders, is really important. The challenges that still exist for women inside and outside the workplace are so pervasive and insidious that you have to take extra care not to just perpetuate them but also to prevent them. When my daughter was 2 days old, I was summoned to a business dinner. We were brand-new parents, and I was dragged out for three hours. It was a watershed moment for me. I'm never putting myself in that position again. I've evolved and become more confident in my own position. I know that family is the most important thing, not what's happening at 6 p.m. in an office."

—PADDY SPENCE, CEO OF ZEVIA, A ZERO-CALORIE DRINK COMPANY

"Our show asks for a lot of toughness that typically isn't assumed or expected of a woman. I had one interaction with a director once, where I was told to protect a female character. I was like, 'No, I'm not. Why would I be protecting her? She can protect herself.' Women don't need saving all the time. All the women on our show are badasses, and they can protect themselves."

—STEVEN YEUN, ACTOR, *THE WALKING DEAD*

Make Your Passion Pay Off

Got a hobby you like way more than your actual job? Whether it's performing, competing, or designing, we can help turn the thing you secretly obsess about at work into the thing you get paid to do.

BY JUDITH OHIKUARE

Dance

PAYAL KADAKIA, FOUNDER OF CLASSPASS AND
ARTISTIC DIRECTOR AT SA DANCE COMPANY

"I started learning Indian folk dance when I was 3 years old and by the time I was 5, I was dreaming up choreography alone in my room. It was like I could see people dancing in my head. Still, I was also very analytical. I attended MIT for undergrad and studied physics and operations management. Even though business seemed more practical, I took classes in the history of dance—I always wanted to stay connected.

"After graduation, I moved to New York to take a job at a global consulting firm and found a dance teacher online who was leading a Bollywood group. *Slumdog Millionaire* had come out and everyone wanted Bollywood performers, so we got asked to do amazing gigs around the city. Then three years later and two months into my next job working on digital strategy at Warner Bros., I assembled a group of dancer friends to work on choreography. That was the beginning of my dance company, Sa Dance. We put on a sold-out showcase, and that summer, we ended up on the cover of the *New York Times* arts section.

"I started to feel like I was having an identity crisis. I wasn't being my best self at either place. Finally, my mom told me to quit. Once she said that, the wheels started turning in my head about all the things I could potentially do. I started Sa to keep dance and fitness in my life, and I started ClassPass to share that experience with other people. Yes, I'm an entrepreneur, but the reason this was all created is because I'm an artist and an inventor—I invent products that make other people happy."

HOW TO BREAK IN: Even though Kadakia felt that she could do well at anything she set her mind to, she needed to bet on dance full-time—without banking on other options—to really make the switch. "Quitting never even crossed my mind until my mom suggested it because I didn't know how to say no," she says. "Then I realized that I wouldn't have time to keep dancing and be a good performer if I was always sitting behind a desk. Everyone else knew I prioritized dance, but I had to say it was a priority or it always would have been the last thing I did."

PAYAL KADAKIA OF CLASSPASS AND SA DANCE
COMPANY IS AN ARTIST NINE-TO-FIVE.

OTHER JOBS FOR DANCE LOVERS

1. Movement therapist
2. Dance teacher
3. Gym/wellness center director
4. Arts manager

"I'm reminded daily of the power of dance and the arts to transform lives."

— KELLY LAMB POLLOCK,
EXECUTIVE DIRECTOR,
THE CENTER OF CREATIVE
ARTS IN ST. LOUIS

Coffee

MICHELLE SUNDQUIST, LEAD BEVERAGE DEVELOPER AT STARBUCKS

OTHER JOBS FOR BEVERAGE LOVERS

1. Wine buyer
2. Beer flavor engineer
3. Food stylist
4. Tea blender

"My grandmother showed me the healing properties of plants. Now, I soothe my passion for healing by blending teas for others."

—ZHENA MUZYKA, FOUNDER OF ZHENA'S GYPSY TEA

"I fell in love with coffee when I was 19 and working at a busy little espresso stand at Crystal Mountain Ski Resort in Seattle. I was surprised to realize that even if you do know how to make coffee, you can still sometimes make it wrong. I spent a lot of time at Crystal Mountain learning about ingredients, the perfect way to steam milk, what makes a good shot of espresso, and how to incorporate flavor. Eventually, I worked my way up the ranks at Seattle's Best before joining the research and development team at Starbucks.

"I work with a team of 10 people that includes managers, culinary experts, and food scientists. We do a ton of flavor exploration, meet with vendors to find out about new ingredients, and dig into trends. We also brainstorm the customer experience. With cold brew, for example, we want to give people a sophisticated experience, whereas with mocha coconut, a flavor we're reintroducing, we discussed whether we want customers to have an indulgent dessert experience, a relaxing vacation escape, or a morning energy boost. I learn something new every day.

"It's kind of funny—even away from the office, the first thing I want to do is find the local Starbucks and see what it's like."

HOW TO BREAK IN:

Sundquist completed three years of college as a drama major before leaving school to join Seattle's Best. She is now earning her certification in food science. She says that focusing on her path and gaining qualifications along the way—rather than delaying action until she felt like an expert—has helped her achieve her goals. "When you're passionate about something, don't be afraid to pursue that opportunity because you don't have the right degree," she says. "Break down your goal into little steps, and become an expert at each thing to get where you want to be."

Sports

CHARLOTTE JONES ANDERSON, EXECUTIVE VICE PRESIDENT AND CHIEF BRAND
OFFICER FOR THE DALLAS COWBOYS

"My family has always been involved in football. My father coached my brother while I cheered on the sidelines. I've also always loved fashion and producing shows, and oddly enough, I get to do both things in this job. The Cowboys are the only team in the NFL that does its own merchandising, which means we manufacture, produce, and retail everything. I've helped design a watch with Hublot and started a partnership with Victoria's Secret Pink. Half the fanbase is female, but breaking through the traditional image of football to push something as simple as a cuter T-shirt has been a challenge.

"More than 160 women work in our organization, and so many skill sets come into play, whether it's food, technology, or medicine. A pivotal point in my career was when I helped negotiate a partnership with the Salvation Army for our Thanksgiving halftime show. We've raised $2 billion, which showed me how much our business decisions can affect fans. The best part of my job is working for something that millions of people have a shared passion for."

HOW TO BREAK IN: Anderson often interviews women looking to work for the NFL. Whether new hires start in marketing and sales or write for the Cowboys' women-focused website, 5 Points Blue, the franchise values energy, innovative thinking, and teamwork. "A lot of people come here hoping to see a player walk down the hall," she says. "They're easy to weed out as opposed to people who want to develop their own talent."

OTHER JOBS FOR SPORTS LOVERS

1. Physical therapist
2. Sports journalist or commentator
3. Data analyst
4. Event organizer

"Even if you cross the finish line 50 times, it feels great. I love that our Rock'n'Roll running series gives people a sense of achievement and takes their fitness to the next level."

—MOLLY QUINN, SVP OF PARTNERSHIP SALES AT COMPETITOR GROUP

Music

ALEXANDRA PATSAVAS, MUSIC SUPERVISOR

OTHER JOBS FOR MUSIC LOVERS

1. Festival promoter

2. Talent booker for television shows

3. Audio engineer/ music producer

4. Music service executive

"I wake up excited about creating new ways to get our 1,400 employees to volunteer and how I can use Spotify to empower more people through music."

— KERRY STEIB, DIRECTOR OF SOCIAL GOOD AT SPOTIFY

"I work to select the music for films like *Twilight* and TV shows like *The O.C.*, *Gossip Girl*, *Grey's Anatomy*, and *How to Get Away With Murder*. It's a dream job since I grew up transfixed by rock and pop.

"When I went to the University of Illinois at Urbana-Champaign, I joined the group that brought acts to campus. That was the first time it occurred to me that music was a business. After college, I moved to Los Angeles and started working in the mail room of a talent agency—not the sexiest of professions but a pretty classic start in entertainment. After about seven months, I joined Broadcast Music Inc., a music-rights management company, as an assistant to the VP in the film and TV department. I organized meetings between composers and my bosses and learned about copyrights. I couldn't believe this job existed.

"When scripts for a show come in, I pitch the creative team songs to accompany scenes, or my team might suggest alternatives to songs in a script. Sometimes, we license preexisting music, and on other projects, like the *Twilight* sequels, we work with artists to create original songs.

"The foremost consideration is how the music pairs with the picture to tell a story. Executive producers and directors make those decisions, and ultimately, it's not about your individual record collection or favorite songs. Working on a period show like *Mad Men* or a procedural like *Criminal Minds* expands my horizons. On *Scandal*, we go for great Motown classics.

"I still get a little thrill any time I license Radiohead. My work has reconfirmed my appreciation for the artists I listened to when I first got into music. I guess they're my first loves."

HOW TO BREAK IN: Collaboration is key, says Patsavas. "Many colleges have great film and media departments," she says. "The best way to learn is to work with a director and experiment. You'll learn how musical vocabulary works and understand what a director or producer is expressing when she says 'I want this to be aggressive' or 'I want this to be heartfelt.' That can mean something different for every person."

Design

DANIELLE ARPS, INTERIOR DESIGNER FOR START-UPS

"My undergrad thesis was in watercolors, and I minored in music. I played the jazz bass. My dad said, 'What are you going to do with that?' and he suggested that I go to grad school for interior design at the Pratt Institute. I'm not good at starving, so it seemed like a good idea.

"I later landed a part-time job with a company I interned for in school, which led to a full-time position with Rita Konig, a former editor at *Domino* magazine who became a mentor to me. She taught me about color, styling, fabrics, and accessories and helped me develop my own aesthetic. I've come to think of interior design as a 3-D sculpture. Like an art installation, design makes people feel a certain way about the space they're in.

"After briefly working at a midsize firm that specializes in high-end hospitality design, I decided to start my own company. I signed up with Homepolish, a company that matches individuals and businesses with interior designers. Through them, I designed offices for Codecademy and Sailthru. Soon, I got referrals to other start-ups. Most of my clients are just starting out, so I advise them to come to me before they sign a lease. I can advise them on building rules and codes. My job is to work with them when they're smaller until they have a budget that will allow us to design their space to the nines. For example, I worked with Gilt on their first office, a warehouse space that the founders wanted to have an industrial feel. Now we're planning their new Manhattan headquarters, which is going for mid-century modern glam.

"I love that my clients trust me, and it feels awesome when they love the end result. It makes my day to make their day."

HOW TO BREAK IN: One of Arps' big breaks came when a former classmate shared a Facebook post about the start-up General Assembly looking for an office designer. And many clients discover her work on Instagram. If you go into design, think of your social accounts and sites as unofficial portfolios. Keep them sleek and updated.

OTHER JOBS FOR DESIGN LOVERS

1. Video-game developer
2. Furniture maker
3. Digital-brand manager
4. Jewelry designer

"Part of being successful in my job is maintaining a curious eye. I travel the world to get new visual inspiration, which makes life exciting!"

—BLYTHE HARRIS, COCREATOR AND CHIEF CREATIVE OFFICER AT STELLA & DOT

You Got the Job! Now What?

READY TO CRUSH YOUR NEW JOB? THAT GIANT BINDER YOU GOT AT ORIENTATION CAN ONLY TAKE YOU SO FAR. HERE'S YOUR COSMO EMPLOYEE HANDBOOK, FULL OF TRUE FACTS THE NICE LADY IN HR IS NEVER, EVER GOING TO TELL YOU.

WOW YOUR BOSS

UNLESS YOUR NEW JOB TITLE IS DUCHESS OF CAMBRIDGE OR DICTATOR OF A SMALL COUNTRY, YOU REPORT TO SOMEONE. MAKE THAT PERSON'S LIFE AS EASY AS POSSIBLE FROM DAY ONE, AND ONLY GOOD THINGS WILL HAPPEN FOR YOU.

1. FIGURE OUT WHAT MATTERS.
How? Just ask, says Alexandra Levit, author of *New Job, New You*. Tell your manager you want to make sure you meet expectations. What would success look like to her? Ideally, during your first meeting, you can get in writing the goals on which you'll be evaluated during your first three months, six months, and year. "The more subjective you leave this, the more open your performance is to interpretation," Levit says.

2. KNOW WHO YOU REPLACED.
You'll want to do some subtle snooping about your predecessor. Ask coworkers about how previous projects worked out—being mindful not to make it about people, which can sound gossipy, but about their job duties, says Levit. You can also directly ask your boss about this, says Anita Bruzzese, author of *45 Things You Do That Drive Your Boss Crazy*. Say, "Is there anything you'd like to see me do in this job that maybe wasn't done before? Is there something you really liked about the person who had this job before me that I can continue to do?" That way, you're not asking anyone to trash-talk a former employee.

3. HAVE A "COMMUNICATION" TALK.
Within the first 90 days of a job, set aside some time with your new manager (or each manager, if you have more than one) to go over some ground rules, says Lindsey Pollak, author of *Becoming the Boss*. How does she want to hear from you? In person? E-mail? Text? If you're running late, what is the best way to tell her? It may seem like small stuff, but keeping the lines of communication running smoothly—and not inadvertently peeving her with long voicemails or weekend e-mails—can get you off to a great start.

WIN OVER YOUR CO-WORKERS

BE HONEST: THE OFFICE IS BASI-CALLY HIGH SCHOOL, AND BEING THE NEW KID IS PAINFUL. YOU'RE NOT SURE WHO HATES WHOM, AND YOU DEFINITELY AREN'T GUARANTEED A FRIEND TO HANG WITH AT LUNCH.

1. DON'T HIDE OUT. If you wait too long to ask people's names and duties, it might feel awkward, says Bruzzese. Ask your manager to make intros, especially to helpful people in roles like office management and accounting.

2. SHOW OFF FRESH IDEAS. A foolproof way to annoy new coworkers: pitching ideas they have tried—or discarded— before. Ask about what's been done. And don't try to blow everything up, even if you inherited a hot mess. "While it can be tempting to come in like gangbusters and prove yourself, being a good listener is a hugely valuable skill," says Levit. Look for a single process or project where you can shine.

3. BE AS NICE TO THE CUSTODIAN AS YOU ARE TO THE CEO. People notice how you treat other people, and some workers have more influence than you think, says Bruzzese. If you rub gatekeepers the wrong way, good luck getting help with the jammed copier, much less face time with anyone important. It doesn't have to be a big deal: If you pass the front desk and notice a package needs to be delivered, say, "Hey, I'm headed that way. Can I drop this off for you?"

4. DON'T PLAY FAVORITES. Know a little bit about a lot of people, instead of joining yourself at the hip with one. You've been cast in a long-running show, and there's a lot of backstory to catch up on. "I learned this the hard way at a previous job," says Sara Nelson, editorial director of Amazon.com and Kindle. "The person who took me under her wing was the office complainer, the person nobody wanted to be stuck with in the elevator. I eventually extricated myself from her, but we never had a normal working relationship after that. She was mad at me for rejecting her, when I should have waited to 'accept' her in the first place."

LOOK LIKE YOU KNOW WHAT YOU ARE DOING

THEY CHOSE YOU FOR THE JOB. YOU ARE NOT A FRAUD. YOU WILL NOT EMBARRASS YOURSELF. (BUT MAYBE TAKE THESE PRECAUTIONS JUST IN CASE.)

1. LEARN THE CULTURE. Here's where you realize that Anthropology 101 seminar was not a total waste. One of the best things you can do at a new job is observe: when people arrive and depart, how people socialize (in the kitchen? over drinks?) and communicate (do people curse? is there a Gchat you should join?). Not to say you have to eat salad at your desk every day just because everyone else does, but know what's normal.

2. TAKE NOTES. People see it as a huge sign of respect when you write down what they are saying and a sign of disrespect when you have to ask again because you didn't write it down. Carry a notebook or your phone. Bruzzese suggests saying, "I'm just going to jot down some notes on my phone so I don't forget the specifics." That way no one thinks you're texting your BF.

3. ADMIT YOUR IGNORANCE. Being asked a direct question on a topic you know nothing about is an unpleasant feeling...but trying to fake your way through an entire conversation on said topic is the stuff of nightmares. Confidence means saying simply, "I haven't heard about that. Can you catch me up?" or "Can you remind me who that is?" During those first 90 days, it's fine to ask a lot of questions, says Pollak.

4. BUT DON'T ADVERTISE YOUR IGNORANCE. Do not, however, ask things you can easily find out elsewhere. "Years ago, I had just started a job and was in a big meeting," says Alexis Bryan Morgan, director of designer relations for Rent the Runway. "Someone mentioned a famous designer, and I blurted out 'Who's that?' My boss looked

at me and joked 'You're fired.' The point is, I should have gone back to my desk and figured it out. Even today, there are so many acronyms in the digital world that are new to me, but instead of wasting everyone's time, I make sure I listen, take notes, and do my homework."

PROTECT YOUR REP

YOU'RE FAMILIAR WITH THE PITFALLS OF THE REPLY ALL FUNCTION, RIGHT? JUST CHECKING.

1. SILENCE YOUR SOCIAL MEDIA. In the beginning, step away from Twitter, Instagram, Facebook, and all your other networks. (When you share that viral video, it carries a time stamp.) And quiet your cell too, says Levit. Moms have a way of blowing up your phone in week one.

2. GET IN EARLY, STAY LATE. "At least in the beginning, try to get there 15 minutes early, and stay about 30 minutes later than your boss," says Bruzzese. Thankfully, face time is less important than it was in the past, at least in some careers. But in a new job, it looks bad to zoom out.

3. PROJECT COMPETENCE. You may not realize it, but body language—and actual language—speaks volumes. "I've worked with people who didn't give enough thought to how they spoke—saying things like yeah, uh-huh, um—as well as offering limp handshakes. It all can translate into immaturity," says Rebecca Widness, founder of Widness and Company Public Relations in New York. Being super-polished with little things like your posture, your outfit, or the way you answer your phone can make you appear (and actually be) more confident.

4. SIP, DON'T SWIG. It's never a great idea to get blitzed with coworkers, but definitely not in the very beginning. Laurie Ruettimann, an HR consultant in Raleigh, North Carolina, recalls how, in an effort to keep up with the guys on her team who took her out to dinner after her first day at work, she helped polish off six bottles of wine. "I ended up puking at 8 p.m. and had to get up the next day for meetings," she says.

5. WHEN IN DOUBT, DON'T. Not sure if you should wear that skirt? Don't. Take that long lunch hour, even if it's a slow day? Don't. Always respect that squiggle of doubt, Pollak says, "especially during those crucial first few months on the job."

SEVEN WAYS YOU SCREWED UP YOUR BENEFITS

IS YOUR APPROACH TO OPEN ENROLLMENT "EENY MEENY MINY MOE"? COSMO FINANCIAL COLUMNIST ALEXA VON TOBEL, CEO OF LEARNVEST AND AUTHOR OF *FINANCIALLY FEARLESS*, GIVES YOU A DO-OVER.

1. YOU OPTED OUT. Take advantage of your perks—life, dental, and especially health insurance—to protect yourself and your finances. (If you don't get benefits through a job, head to HealthCare.gov.) I opted out of a $7 per month dental plan at my first job . . . only to get a cavity and a huge bill!

2. YOU PICKED THE WRONG PLAN. Consider the true cost of a health plan: not only monthly premiums but also copays, prescriptions, deductibles (how much you pay before the plan kicks in), and coinsurance (the percentage you cover after it kicks in). Look for a plan with a lower deductible, especially if you have a chronic health issue, see a specialist, take brand-name meds, or might get pregnant. Consider high out-of-pocket costs only if you're healthy and can't afford better coverage. But remember, anyone can get sick or injured, and one trip to the ER can cost a lot.

3. YOU RE-UPPED WITHOUT THINKING.
Ninety percent of workers auto-enroll in the same health plan each year, a 2014 study by Aflac found. The best way to prepare for the unknown is to review your benefits and make sure they still fit your needs.

4. YOU DIDN'T TEAM UP.
If you live with a partner, you might save by becoming a dependent on your S.O.'s insurance (or vice versa). Plus, people under 26 can glom onto a parent's insurance. Be aware of differing open-enrollment periods.

5. YOU PRETENDED YOU'D NEVER GET OLD.
You're going to work for roughly 50 years to support 70(ish) years of your life—the earlier you start saving for retirement, the better. Aim to contribute at least 5 percent of your base salary monthly by age 25 and 10 percent by age 30 to an employer-sponsored 401(k). If you're not enrolled at work, try a Roth IRA, which you can open online. Don't touch a penny in your retirement accounts before age $59\frac{1}{2}$ to avoid a major hit from taxes and penalties.

6. YOU NEGLECTED YOUR MONEY.
Just because you won't use your retirement money soon doesn't mean you should ignore it. Set a calendar alert to check on your investments at least once a year—as you get older, you'll want to take less risk. Brokerage firms have free online retirement calculators that can help you find a good mix. And keep an eye on those funds after you leave your job. If you feel unorganized, combining all your retirement accounts into one (aka rolling them over) might help.

7. YOU LEFT BENEFITS BEHIND.
Perks don't always vanish as soon as you give notice or lose your job. Drop by HR to ask if any benefits will linger. In some cases, a severance package can be negotiated to extend your health and dental plans temporarily. Some companies will provide at least 18 months of COBRA insurance—but you cover the (high) cost.

THE WEIRD PEOPLE YOU MEET AT WORK

CHERISH YOUR NORMAL, RESPECTFUL CO-WORKER... BUT BE READY FOR THESE GUYS TOO.

THE POISON PILL

She hates her job, and the only thing that appears to cheer her up is making you hate yours too.

WHEN YOU'RE AROUND ONE

A key virtue of starting a new job is hope, so don't let anyone drain yours, says Ross McCammon, author of *Works Well With Others*. Ignore her messages, or rebuff her with a quick, "Sorry, super busy!"

THE CREEPY OLD DUDE

He is wearing a wedding ring but likes to walk up to you from behind and whisper.

WHEN YOU'RE AROUND ONE

Be direct. Tell him you have no interest in what he's doing. Try: "I'd like to preserve this working relationship, but I'd appreciate if you would stop." If he persists, talk to a manager.

SHOUTY MCGEE

She needs to express every thought, loudly.

WHEN YOU'RE AROUND ONE

She might be anxious or excited. Try being empathetic ("It sounds like you have something intense going on . . .") or playful ("Wow! You. Are. Talking. Really. Loud!"). Either way, says McCammon, "deal with it really early on. It's awkward, but it's worse if you let it fester and become passive-aggressive." (Upside: Loud talkers might be a shouting helpful scoop.)

THE SMUG SEXIST

Excels at mansplanations and discounts all your ideas until another man endorses them.

WHEN YOU'RE AROUND ONE

Stop him with a firm "Thanks, Chad, but I know that. Here's what I'd really like to get to." This moves the convo along and lets people know what you know.

THE GHOST

You need her input desperately. But she's never at her desk.

WHEN YOU'RE AROUND ONE

Face-to-face convos are more efficient than e-mail with elusive types, McCammon says: "As soon as she walks in, pop in and start talking." Give her a quick list of things you need answered, then go through it item by item, and lastly, sum up what you plan to do.

SILENT BUT JUDGE-Y

He's definitely feeling things about your work, but he's not communicating.

WHEN YOU'RE AROUND ONE

Are you sure this is about you? He could be annoyed at something else entirely or have a case of Resting Douche Face. Approach him by saying, "I've noticed that when I do this, you do this."

THE PRANKSTER

He thinks he's the next coming of Jim Halpert. You think he's unfunny and distracting.

WHEN YOU'RE AROUND ONE

Don't feel you need to engage, even if it makes you feel a little like a jerk. "Non-response when someone is joking can be really powerful," McCammon says. "You drain the situation of the energy he tried to put into it." Be glad he's too busy with his act to outshine you on the job.

THE GUY WHO GETS AWAY WITH EVERYTHING

He comes to work late, passes off assignments, and still gets promoted.

WHEN YOU'RE AROUND ONE

Watch and learn—he might have something to teach you. "He's figured something out," McCammon says. "There is something he brings to the table that the boss loves." Let him do whatever he's doing, and focus on adding your own value.

How to Stand Up to Anybody

MEGYN KELLY FEARS NO MAN (OR WOMAN). THE FORMER ATTORNEY TURNED GUTSY FOX NEWS CHANNEL ANCHOR, 44, TELLS HOW TO TURN TENSE WORK SITUATIONS INTO OPPORTUNITIES.

REMEMBER IT'S JUST YOUR JOB

In my private life, I hate confrontation! It's precarious ground negotiating private relationships with people you care about. But when I have my professional gear on, I've always felt more empowered. In my line of work, you are expected to confront. If I ever have a contentious interview and I find out that the guest was unhappy, I'll go to them and say, "Look, this is my job. If you're gonna come on prime time at the Fox News Channel, where we have to cover a lot in three minutes, it's going to have to be hardhitting. If you can't handle that, you shouldn't be here." I've had to rise to that occasion, too, as the host.

PICK YOUR BATTLES

When I was fresh out of law school at age 25, I was the only female lawyer in our office. My boss kept asking me to copy cases for him, and he never asked the male lawyers. I resolved that I would confront him. I planned exactly what I would say, which took away some of the nerves. I said, "If you want me to make a copy and come in and have a discussion as lawyers, I'll do that, but I won't copy that case for you." I saw him go red in the face and he started yelling, and it was a scary moment. My heart was pounding. I was worried I was about to be fired on the spot. But I had planned my follow-up too. I said, "Bob, if you want to speak to me like a professional, then we can have that conversation. Otherwise, this conversation is over for now." He was so mad, he wound up calling the head partners of the firm. They told him, "Not only is she right, but we don't ever want to hear about your asking an associate of this law firm to copy cases again." It was so important for me. You only need to do that once, and forevermore you have that power. And as for my old boss Bob, he and I went on to coauthor articles and try cases together, because I had earned his respect.

DON'T MAKE YOURSELF A VICTIM

We all know people who make everything into a confrontation and walk around as victims. Other than cruelty, I can't think of anything much more unattractive than making yourself into a victim. And women do it too often. They chalk up their lack of a pro-

motion or the advancement of someone else to their own bad luck. They lash out at someone for being unfair to them as opposed to asking, How can I change the situation? What did I do that led me into this situation? How can I stop doing that and get better results?

MATCH THEIR ENERGY

As a first-year lawyer, I learned how to mirror other people's body language, and it really works. If somebody comes in upset and fired up saying, "What happened?!" it is totally inappropriate for you to say, "I don't know. I'm very sorry," in a low voice. You have to say firmly, "You're right! That should not have happened, and I'm on it!" And vice versa, you might need to take it down a notch if that person is down a notch. Just by matching the other person's energy and delivery, you make them feel heard and validated. Of course, if I had an opposing counsel who was trying to pummel me, I would not try to mirror them, because they were an adversary. I would calmly say, "You seem upset. Do you need to take a break?" Oh, they hated that. And I loved it.

GIVE IT A MINUTE

Whenever anybody phones you angry, give it as much time as you reasonably can before you return the call. Think about when you're the person who is angry: You fire off something in an e-mail or there's a phone call. And then an hour or two passes, and you're like, all right, it wasn't that big of a deal. Or something will happen in the interim to bring it down. I can tell you, I've saved myself so many times by doing that.

KEEP THE FOCUS ON YOU

Whether it's a work confrontation or a breakup, you may spend weeks obsessing about the other guy. Did I screw that up? Did I say the wrong thing? Am I what he wants? But you're focusing on the wrong person. It's not whether he likes you, it's whether you like him. It's about whether he did the right thing toward you. All the energy we put into contentious relationships, if you funnel all that energy back into yourself, everything works out. You become a more interesting person, you attract the right people into your life, and life gets better for you.

3

LOVE,
LUST
&
OTHER
STUFF

Refresh Your Friendventory

It's cocktail o'clock, but what if a big move landed you a plane ride away from your go-to BFFs? It's time to meet some new girls to bond with. Here's your cheat sheet.

YOU MOVED CROSS-COUNTRY to kick ass at your dream job...or move in with your guy. The only thing missing from your adventurous new chapter is your posse.

"The 20s and 30s are a time of intense transitions—moving, taking new jobs, starting romantic relationships or families," says psychologist Andrea Bonior, PhD, author of *The Friendship Fix: The Complete Guide to Choosing, Losing, and Keeping Up With Your Friends*. According to a (kinda sad!) study from the Netherlands Organization for Scientific Research, we lose about half our friends every seven years. Womp.

If your social circle is shrinking, act like you would postbreakup: Shed your sweatpants, get back out there, and meet some new (girl) crushes. Yes, making new friends as a grown-ass woman can be intimidating (especially if you're not on a campus swarming with potential BFFs anymore). But chances are, there are already cool girls in your life right now. Take a cue from these success stories of casual acquaintances who became legit friends. The Rachel to your Monica is out there...so go out and find her!

THE FELLOW GYM RAT

She's the cool girl rocking out on the treadmill next to you. But how do you go from sweaty smiles to postworkout drinks, er, green juice?

▸ **SHE MADE IT WORK** After struggling to adjust her Spinning bike at a new gym in a new city, Jayne Miller, 24, looked at Barb and asked, "'Do you have any idea how to do this?' The next time we met in class, we exchanged numbers and a mutual 'We should hang out.' We both instantly felt that girlfriend connection."

▸ **YOUR GAME PLAN** "Show vulnerability," says life coach Shasta Nelson, author of *Friendships Don't Just Happen*. It's easier to relate when you're not perfect.

THE COOL COWORKER

You see each other every day, you have similar career goals, and frankly, you both need someone with whom to recap *The Mindy Project*.

▸ **SHE MADE IT WORK** Amina Ray, 34, was a new hire at a Chicago law firm when she hit it off with fellow attorney

Allison. "We were both single and shared a love of pinot noir," Ray says. They started getting lunch, but "one night when we were stuck late at work, I asked her to get dinner. A year and a half later, Allison introduced me to my husband… and was in my wedding."

▶ **YOUR GAME PLAN** Going straight from midday meetings to Saturday night dance parties may feel like a drastic jump, so start with workday hangs. Eventually, a Sunday brunch invite will feel totally natural.

THE BOOK CLUB/ RUNNING CLUB GAL

You already share an interest—half marathons, Jhumpa Lahiri—now it's just a matter of taking your occasional woman dates to the next level.

▶ **SHE MADE IT WORK** When Kate Eisenpress, 25, joined a book club in Lake Village, Arkansas, she was happy to have an interesting way to meet new friends. "We talked about reading, but conversation eventually turned to what we were doing over the weekend," Kate says. "We started having coffee dates, and today, some of my book-club ladies are my closest friends."

▶ **YOUR GAME PLAN** Exploit common interests. If you bonded big-time over your love of *Night Film*, she's probably down for a David Fincher movie date.

THE FRIEND OF A FRIEND

Meeting a potential bestie through a mutual friend comes with a major perk— she's already been prescreened by someone you love and trust.

▶ **SHE MADE IT WORK** Phoebe Lapine, 28, met most of her circle in New York through mutual pals who were cool enough to invite her to birthday parties and happy hours. "I have an entire group of friends I call my city friends. We just connected through friends of friends, and now we're a crew of our own," she says.

▶ **YOUR GAME PLAN** Embrace the group hang, including your mutual friend whenever possible to avoid potential drama.

Happy Friendiversary!

Anniversaries aren't just for lovahs anymore.
Raise your glass and celebrate the date you met
the most important person in your life—your BFF.

"NO DIGGITY," the '90s jam by Blackstreet, pours out of the speakers at New York City's Bob Bar, where Leela Hatfield, 27, and her best friend, Alie Martell, 27, are throwing a party. Nostalgia is already in the air: The pair are wearing custom-made tank tops recreating their childhood Best Friends charm necklaces and handing out stickers emblazoned with their smiling faces and a special hashtag: #Since1993.

Their guests shower them with gifts (they thought about registering but thought that would be greedy) and cards—one starring two poodles and a message reading, "Happy Anniversary, you two amazing bitches!"

Welcome to Alie and Leela's 20-year friendiversary party, a giggle- and gin-infused affair marking two decades since Martell showed up as the new girl at Hatfield's elementary school, bonded with her over a shared love of Easy Bake Ovens, and became her sister from another mister. "I've been best friends with Alie for almost my entire life, and it's a big deal," Hatfield says. "Friendship milestones are usually overlooked, but we wanted to celebrate our anniversary and share it with all our friends." Martell agrees: "We're used to people posting their anniversary flowers on Facebook, but it feels like more of an achievement to celebrate having been friends for so long."

With more women getting married later in life (the average age of a first-time bride in the U.S. has crept up from 25 to around 27) and a longer stretch of our lives consumed with roommate bonding and seeing each other through breakups and new jobs, girlfriends are closer than ever. For the new breed of Tina-and-Amy-tight besties, friendiversaries are a way to acknowledge their true partners in life—their BFFs.

FRIENDIVERSARY FEVER

"The idea of celebrating your friendship has grown steadily," says Jan Yager, PhD, author of *Friendshifts: The Power of*

Friendship and How It Shapes Our Lives. Considering the high divorce rate, she notes, romantic anniversaries seem dicier, while the number of friendship greeting cards at drugstores has blown up over the last several years. Fox's *New Girl* helped spark the trend when Schmidt and Nick feted their 10-year friendiversary with a lavish garden party in season two. Now #Friendiversary is a familiar presence on Twitter, with tweets shouting out photo albums and dinners.

Chavie Lieber, 24, a writer, recently hosted four former coworkers-turned-besties for a mimosa-soaked three-year-friendiversary brunch at her New York apartment. The group, which calls itself The Assistants Club, began bonding over "bitch work" three years ago, and although they've all moved on to new (and more senior) jobs, they're closer than ever.

"We feel it's important to mark the time that we

MARTELL (LEFT) AND
HATFIELD PUT RACHEL
AND MONICA TO SHAME.

123

became friends," says Nora Barak, 26, a social-media editor. "Not to be so Carrie Bradshaw, but we're all 20something women trying to make it big and we're all supporting each other."

"I don't have a boy to celebrate an anniversary with, so I'm very happy to be celebrating my friendiversary," says Ann Wermiel, 25, a photographer. But even her friend Beryl Shereshewsky, 28, a freelance video producer who just celebrated her two-year anniversary with her boyfriend, confesses: "I was way more excited waking up this morning for our friendiversary. I literally waited in line to buy fancy juices for mimosas for 30 minutes. I would never do that for my boyfriend!"

BFF-DOM IN THE DIGITAL AGE

It may seem ironic that friendiversaries are cropping up at a time when we're more likely to Gchat our friends than call them and long-standing dinner plans are routinely broken via last-minute texts. But when friends do keep it together, it's all the more reason to throw a party.

"Some friends, rather than tell me personally that they're not going to make it to my birthday party, just send a quick Facebook message," says Kelly Thom, 30. But her BFF Libby Piller, 31, never flakes via text. The inseparable pair toasted each other with bourbon and "strong chick music," like Miranda Lambert, at the stroke of midnight at their one-year friendiversary bash at an Oshkosh, Wisconsin, bar last November. "Libby and I both trust that the other person will be there when it's important."

Separated by a two-hour drive in northern England, British fashion blogger Annie Moss, 29, and her best friend from college, Jodi Kelly, 28, keep in touch through Twitter—but meeting for a 10-year friendiversary weekend in London last October was the perfect way to catch up in the flesh over gossip and French martinis. Ten years earlier, they clicked over a shared passion for fashion. When they showed up to London's Dirty Martini bar, "OMGs" rang out as they realized they were both wearing wild statement pants and nude pumps.

"When you have a friend who you haven't spoken to in months and the conversation just picks up where it left off, it really is something to celebrate," Moss says. "It's respecting that some friendships don't always last, but with Jodi, I've got a best friend for life."

Back in New York, the morning after Hatfield and Martell's 20th friendiversary, the duo (who live together, natch) were already contemplating their 30th friendiversary party. "People come and go," Hatfield says. "Alie's forever."

1 MOSS AND KELLY DO LONDON. 2 WERMIEL, SHERESHEWSKY, LAUREN BUCKLEY, BARAK, AND LIEBER. 3 THOM AND PILLER ROCK THEIR FRIENDIVERSARY BASH. 4 THE ASSISTANTS CLUB'S SUMMER FIELD TRIP TO UPSTATE NEW YORK.

Can Your MOM Be Your BFF?

In best-selling author Jodi Picoult's novel, *Leaving Time*, a daughter searches for clues about her long-lost mom. But in real life, Picoult and daughter Samantha van Leer, 19, are BFF-level close. Here are their tips for keeping a strong bond.

KNOW WHEN TO BE FRIENDS

SAMMY: I think there's a time to be a mom and a time to be a friend. She seems more human because she can turn on and off the mom-dar. Like when we're shopping together, she knows she doesn't have to act like the overbearing mother—she's a friend. That's when I really see her as a human being, not just an alien mother ship.

JODI: If every time you are with your daughter, you have a fight...or talk about something serious and huge, that's not a relationship. That's militaristic. The relationship crystallizes during all the small moments. The year before you went off to college, we would sit down and watch *Say Yes to the Dress* and just talk. I was like, "My wedding gown is in the attic, and I've never taken it out of its box. You should try it on!" So you tried it on, and swear to god, it was like it was made for you.

SAMMY: Except it was super not in style.

JODI: Well, okay, we're going back to the Princess Di era with the big shoulders...but it was really a fun moment.

BELIEVE YOUR MOM'S COMPLIMENTS

JODI: There are so many negative messages being thrust on young women today: You're not pretty enough; you're not smart enough. And as far as I'm concerned, she's the prettiest, smartest girl out there, so I'm gonna tell her that, and hopefully if I say it often enough, she might start to believe it.

SAMMY: Obviously, I'm going to roll my eyes and be like, "You have to say that; you're my mom." But still, it's one less person saying something negative. I've managed to surround myself with the skinniest, most beautiful friends. So maybe on that day when I look in the mirror and I'm like, "Great, going to the beach with my friends," I hear my mom's voice going, "You look so great!"—and it makes me feel so much better.

JODI: It's true! You're so athletic, and you're an incredible dancer. You couldn't do the things that you do if you didn't have the power in your legs and butt. Your butt is legendary.

LET THE SMALL STUFF ROLL OFF YOUR BACK

JODI: If she's really being an über-bitch, I will call her on it. But there are times too when you pick your battles. When she comes home for the summer and cooks, she uses every pan in the kitchen and does not clean a single one. My husband gets mad, and I'm like, "Whatever, I'll clean the damn pans," because it's just not worth it. Then there are times when I'll say something totally innocuous to you and you take my head off.

SAMMY: My friends talk about how our moms are our PMS punching bags. It's like, something will strike you and they're the one person who just sets it off....

JODI: Honestly, I think it's because we strike out at the people who are closest to us.

SAMMY: And most like us. You're probably mad at yourself for something, and the person who is most like you comes by so you yell at her.

CRACK EACH OTHER UP

JODI: For reasons I still don't understand, Sammy and her two brothers call me Hodor. They stole my phone and made it so that every time I typed the word *a* or *the*, the word *Hodor* [the *Game of Thrones* character] pops up instead. I think it's funny. I know they respect me, and sometimes it's good to just be silly together.

SAMMY: Hodor? What are you saying? All I hear is "Hodor Hodor Hodor."

> ## "When I look in the mirror...I hear my mom's voice going, 'You look so great!'— and it makes me feel so much better."
> —SAMMY VAN LEER

Break Your Bad Guy Habits

LIKE A BRAINWASHED LOVE ZOMBIE, you just can't stop hooking up with the same guys on loop? Oh yes, you can. Whether it's tall, dark, and handsome or deeply damaged, we all have a type...or do we? "A lot of women have this misconception that the 'type' they fall in love with is out of their hands," says Andrea Syrtash, author of *He's Just Not Your Type (and That's a Good Thing)*. Spoiler: Not true! We broke down four classic man ruts we all fall into and how to break out of them like a triumphant rom-com heroine.

THE ASSHOLE

This is the guy who talks his way backstage at a Kanye concert, makes out with you in front of Yeezus himself, doesn't text you again for two months, then wants to go out again like your first date was yesterday. He's totally full of himself yet weirdly charismatic—all at once. "Everyone's attracted to confidence, so it's easy to fall for these guys," says Chiara Atik, author of *Modern Dating: A Field Guide.* Hook up with enough a-holes and you'll find yourself addicted to the challenge. "I've dated nice guys, but I get sick of them in, like, two weeks," says Marisa F., 26. "I guess somehow emotional unavailability came to equal masculinity to me."

▶ **How to Break Out:** Throw a bottle of fancy cologne his way, and when he looks the other way, run! Seriously though, delete the dude from your phone, and the next time he texts you at 2 a.m., write back that you have a boyfriend now—whether or not that's actually true.

▶ **Who to Break Out With:** The Paul Bunyan. He's take-charge, outdoorsy, always taking you on adventures. He packs the excitement of an a-hole, except he actually has hobbies other than trying to get into your pants, then ignoring you.

THE *MEH* BOYFRIEND

This male equivalent of an easy-listening station can be tempting. He's super sweet (like vanilla ice cream). You have a date to bring to weddings! He's nice to your mom! He even sends you flowers for no reason (even if they're never the ones you told him you like). But there's no fire in your loins (he's big on missionary, and that's about it), and you can't stop thinking about that annoying *Sex and the City* episode about zsa zsa zsu....

▶ **How to Break Out:** Consider that "long-term relationships are always going to be a little less exhilarating than a new boyfriend," says Atik. But when you're staying with him only because you're afraid of the alternative (#ForeverAlone), it's time to stop settling for just anyone and get comfortable being solo. Translation: Dump him now.

▶ **Who to Break Out With:** No one! Girl, do you. Go to the movies alone. Go out to dinner alone. It's amazing. Sit at the bar, get a meal, and make friends with someone else there. I seriously still hang out with a girl I met this way. She's super fun, and she has a cool name: Souad. I digress, but the advice stands. It's better to be alone than to settle. Just being out in the world and leaving your comfort zone opens you up to attracting a guy for whom you might actually feel a spark....

THE BAGGAGE MAN

There's something weird lurking in his closet—perhaps a *Breaking Bad*–style secret meth lab? It's all so torturous and passionate—especially in bed—that you resolve to "fix" him. "Women like to think of themselves as the magic key that unlocks the perfect guy inside," Atik explains. Elie S., 25, has been stuck in a rut of emotionally unavailable men for years. "It always seems so exciting," she says. Until his ex pops out of a bush in prison orange....

▶ **How to Break Out:** A more constructive way to tap into your nurturing side? Start volunteering. It'll feel a lot better than dating dudes with rap sheets.

▶ **Who to Break Out With:** The Culture Buff. He's experienced and deep, minus the secret family across state lines.

THE MAN-BOY

Peter Pans are just fun. I dated one once, and we spent so much time singing Sublime in my car that I almost forgot he didn't have a license and lived with his mom. Man-children are so spontaneous, they make you feel like you just pounded three Red Bulls. It's not until you wake up at 10 a.m. on a Wednesday with a throbbing hangover that his devil-may-care-ness loses its charm. Claire M. (not her real name), 32, rebounded from a breakup with a string of Peters, saying they "felt so laid-back" that it seemed they wouldn't hurt her.

▶ **How to Break Out:** Start hanging out where more mature guys do. "Go to events that have to do with your hobbies," says Atik. Ask friends who have their shit together to set you up with proper, functioning adults.

▶ **Who to Break Out With:** The Adventurer. This guy's fun like a Peter Pan, but he has the job and the paid vacation days to back it up. Good-bye, Groupon dates and morning-after breakfasts of Flamin' Hot Cheetos. Hola, cliff diving in Ibiza!

LAST WORD:
The best way to break out of your man rut? Ask yourself why you keep falling for the same duds. Then tell yourself: You deserve better!

This Is NOT Why You're Single

Do your friends and family think they know the reason you're solo? Well, they don't. **Sara Eckel** takes on six of the most common (and lame, judge-y, and simply untrue) reasons women are told they're still single.

WHEN SEARCHING FOR LOVE, it feels like you can't win. You're told that to find a good relationship, you should first be happy alone. But if you are content solo, then you're "too independent." So you admit that being single can be lonely... and are informed that you reek of desperation! Before I met my husband, Mark, my single friends and I would talk about the many theories our loved ones offered up about why we hadn't found someone. They meant well, but now I know they were just plain wrong (I wasn't afraid of commitment; I just hadn't found the right guy!). I talked to so many women about the clueless feedback they hear that I was inspired to write a book—*It's Not You: 27 (Wrong) Reasons You're Single*. Here, why the top "reasons" for why you're single are a bunch of bunk.

Reason no. 1 "You're too intimidating/independent"

Suzanne was a successful communications consultant who owned her own house and a couple of cars. "My male friends told me my life could scare men away, because where is there room for them? They said I needed to look more vulnerable," she says. But the idea that having a spine and a brain will hurt your chance of finding love is baloney. The truth is, women with college degrees and higher incomes are just as likely to marry as their less accomplished peers. They're also less likely to divorce. So instead of trying to squash your spirit to please some insecure dude, why not wait for a guy who has the cojones to cheer when you get a promotion? That's what Suzanne did, and she's now happily married to a confident man—who's more than happy that she shares her house and two cars with him.

WHAT TO SAY BACK "I didn't realize so many guys were such delicate flowers! I think I'll hold out for one who's man enough to date me."

"You're Too Picky"

When I asked women what their friends and family said about why they were alone, this was the overwhelming favorite. It's a nice fail-safe, since it's pretty hard to prove wrong. If he was rude to the waitress last night, maybe he was having a bad day. "Give him another chance!" is the cry of the reasonable.

My single friends and I would puzzle over this: Were our standards too exacting? None of us had salary requirements. We weren't looking for men to support us, although they did need to be able to support themselves. In fact, the only standard that truly mattered to any woman I knew was the one articulated by my friend Caitlin. "I want to find a guy who is as sweet and surprising as my friends are but who I also want to make out with," she said. I have yet to meet a happily coupled person whose significant other fails to clear this bar.

Caitlin did indeed find a guy like this, and they've been happily married for years. But when we were single, this attitude made us nuts—"Are you sure? Why not just go on one more date?"

Here's what we failed to see: Our friends weren't trying to make us feel bad. After all, accusing a single person of being too selective is a compliment in a way. It assumes that scads of people want to be with you.

Plus, there is a reason we got so much feedback. We asked for it...or complained enough that our friends felt compelled to cough up some sort of wisdom. The solution: Stop talking about it. Relying on your own judgment rather than a survey of your 12 closest friends is liberating. You don't have to justify not going on that third OkCupid date if no one knows about the first one.

WHAT TO SAY BACK **"I'm choosing a life partner, not a couch."**

"You Don't Know How to Play the Game"

The media treats dating like a cosmic tennis match in which women are cast as the losers and men are the victors, reveling in their bachelor freedom. That's why there's a tendency for a girl to be on defensive. He postponed a date? Failed to call? Then, sister, you are outta there! How do you know, though, if you're being overly harsh on a guy? For me, the best guide was, How does he make you feel? Does anything he does set off alarm bells? If not, give him the benefit of the doubt. Isn't it braver to "play the game" with an open heart, instead of your main strategy being to prevent it from getting broken?

WHAT TO SAY BACK **"That's because it's not a sport to me—I'm looking for a boyfriend, not a trophy."**

"You Should Have Married That Guy"

Reason no. 4

When Julia broke up with Joe, her mom and sister told her she expected too much from relationships. Julia knew that Joe was a great guy—but she didn't feel a spark, and she refused to settle. Isn't it funny? At the same time women are expected to be superhuman—nailing the perfect balance of sexy yet modest, independent yet vulnerable—we're also supposed to be grateful for any scrap of male attention that comes our way. So what if he's dull in bed? You can't have it all!

Julia worried her standards were too high...until she met Matt, who confirmed that "I wasn't crazy. I knew what this would feel like and was holding out for it!" she says.

Laurie, a TV exec, admits she was pretty exacting: Her future boyfriend would have to love the arts, not be religious, and live in Manhattan. Then she met a hilarious man named Dave—a Christian who lived in the suburbs and couldn't care less about museums. They've been married for 10 years. Did she settle? "Absolutely not! I feel lucky," she says. Laurie's list was off, but her instincts weren't. She finds Dave smart and attractive, and he treats her like the most desirable woman in the world. Who cares if he doesn't dig the symphony? So how do you know if you're settling? Easy. You're settling if you think you're settling.

WHAT TO SAY BACK "I decided that years of quiet desperation followed by divorce just wasn't for me."

"You're Too Available"

Reason no. 5

Rose's relationships typically didn't last long—only three to six months. So she asked her married friends for advice. "They said I was caring too much and not playing hard to get," says Rose. This is classic dating advice: Keep him guessing, because men love the hunt.

This idea is presented as empowering—but in telling women to act like unavailable ice queens, the message is: Hide your true feelings, because if he sees how you really feel, he will leave. How is that supposed to make you feel confident? To Rose, acting bitchy or withholding kindness from a guy she liked just didn't feel right.

So for all of her self-doubt, Rose held onto a small but fierce instinct that one day she'd meet someone who wouldn't need to be manipulated into liking her. She was right. She's now married to a man who adores her… and the fact that she's not afraid to express her feelings.

WHAT TO SAY BACK "I'm a person, not a restaurant reservation. I'm pretty sure there's a guy out there smart enough to know the difference."

Reason no.6

"You Have Issues"

Are you commitment phobic? Afraid of intimacy? Too close to your father? Not close enough? If you're a single woman, the pathologies you're accused of are endless.

There's nothing wrong with working through your issues. If you want to conquer your fear of heights, go for it! The problem arises when you try to eradicate your hang-ups as a prerequisite to finding a relationship. Let's face it: If everyone had to shed their psychological baggage before finding a partner, there would be a lot more unattached people in the world.

What if you stopped defining yourself as someone with a bad-boy addiction or low self-esteem? What if you instead saw yourself as a flawed but lovable human being? What if the only reason you're alone is because you just haven't met the right partner yet?

Sara Eckel is a writer in Kingston, New York, who married her dream guy after years of being single.

WHAT TO SAY BACK

"And you don't?"

SAY WHAT?!

More ludicrous reasons readers have been told they're single.

"Your sense of humor is too dry. Men probably think you're bitchy." —AMY B., 25

"You travel a lot. How's a guy supposed to know when you'll be around?" —SARA R., 25

"You're too close to your family. No man wants to compete with them." —KATIE C., 27

"You're a redhead. Men usually don't marry redheads." —SAMANTHA F., 37

"You're too pretty. Guys would rather marry the less-intimidating girl next door." —CARMEN S., 26

So You're Ready for the DTR Talk

Just remember: Wanting to know where you stand in a relationship doesn't make you clingy or crazy. It just means you want to know if you should stop collecting numbers when you go out on the weekends.

Decide What You Want and What You Don't Want.

If defining the relationship were a one-way street (which, obviously, it isn't), what would your dream outcome be? Even if you're not necessarily looking for a label, go into the conversation knowing what you will and won't settle for. If one of those scenarios is a deal breaker (think: one of you wants to be in an open relationship while the other's trying to put this on lockdown), you may need to walk.

Be Sober and Fully Clothed.

It may seem like downing the better part of a bottle of Sancerre will take the edge off, but being drunk only escalates emotions and will (we promise) make things worse. Same goes for attempting the talk post-sex—that naked cuddle session should be reserved for deciding where you'll get brunch tomorrow, not if he's willing to attend your stepsister's wedding in August.

Go Straight to the Source.

There are really only two people who can define what you're doing: you and him. So don't crowdsource, don't blog about it, don't query his friends or consult your horoscope—just ask him. It can be tempting to do some field reporting first, but ultimately, the only thing that's going to get you real answers is a face-to-face talk with the boy.

Be Direct.

"Subtle hints never work," says Margret L., 23, of Milwaukee, Wisconsin. ("Oh, weird, this RSVP card says Significant Others Welcome. Hmm....") Entering the conversation, you both should know that a DTR is going down.

Keep It Playful.

Don't feel like you have to lead with the grim reaper of conversation starters: "We need to talk." This convo can be lighthearted, so lead with a joke, like: "What's warm and fuzzy but still confusing-as-eff all over?" Answer: "This relationship!" (Insert '90s-sitcom laugh track here.)

Say What You Need to Say.

Time to be articulate! If you initiated the talk, go first explaining how you feel—that way, you won't get caught up in what he says. Sure, it's tempting to see what he's thinking first...but then you might be left with a definition you're not comfortable with.

Listen.

Be ready to hear him out and he'll be more likely to give you an honest answer. And remember: Just because you want to define the relationship doesn't mean it needs to be black and white. Just make sure that if you're going to continue, you're on the same page.

OMG! THAT DID NOT GO WELL!

Chalk this one up to a loss—his loss. There could be a number of reasons why it didn't work out, but none of them are worth your obsessing over and analyzing into a fine powder of agony. The best thing you can do after a bad DTR is whip out your cutest Beyoncé-channeling jeans and let the swarm of eligible Jay-Zs vie for your affection.

WAIT, IT TOTALLY DID!

Hey, girl, way to successfully D that R! Now that you're on the same page, enjoy the newfound bliss of introducing each other at parties with no awkward weirdness whatsoever.

137

First Comes Love, Then Comes... MOVING IN!

From dividing dirty dishes to, ahem, other dirty things to do around your new nest, here's how to make living together feel like home sweet home.

COHABITATION IS THE NEW GETTING ENGAGED.
Almost 50 percent of young women in the U.S. live with a lovah before saying "I do." When should you do it, what does your boyfriend really think about it—and how can a giant cardboard box double as a sex prop? Read on, then pack your bags and change your address to 6969 Love Boulevard.

Guys are twice as likely as women to expect to move in after dating for 6 months (or less), according to Match.com. Easy, guys—let's start with a dresser drawer.

1 If one of you got a job across the country, would you move there with the other?

If you'd live anywhere with this person—because you truly want to take things to the #NextLevel—you should feel good about apartment hunting. But if moving in is about saving rent or ditching lame roommates, think twice. "Cohabiting for convenience may lock you into a relationship that isn't good for you," says W. Bradford Wilcox, PhD, director of the National Marriage Project, at the University of Virginia. He says couples who make intentional decisions about milestones like moving in are more likely to stay together than those who casually "slide" into big transitions because it seems easy. Think about the "woulds" of living together rather than the "shoulds" (i.e., "I'd gladly have this guy in my bed every night" versus "All my friends live with their boyfriends, so I should too").

2 Can we deal with household stuff without hating each other's guts?

A serious concern about his character (he's really selfish) could be a deal breaker. But if you're worried about his habit of leaving crusty chili bowls in the sink, that's totally normal. In fact, 83 percent of women say moving in with a boyfriend or girlfriend for the first time is a "real challenge," and the toughest issue is dividing chores, according to a survey by online art marketplace UGallery. Handle it Olivia Pope–style before move-in day: Order takeout, uncork wine, and divvy future tasks according to your strengths—maybe he's boss at cooking, and you're the lord of dishwasher loading. And plan to "negotiate your personal space," says Samantha Boardman, MD, a clinical instructor in psychiatry at Weill Cornell Medical College. "Having separate drawers and closets provides a sense of autonomy and makes you less likely to freak out when he leaves his towel on the floor." Preach!

3 Are we ready to have a serious chat about money?

It's not the sexiest conversation, but you should be comfortable going there because cosigning a lease is no joke. "If your partner misses a rent payment, that could ding your credit score, since cosigning means you're responsible for any missing money," says Alexa von Tobel, founder and CEO of LearnVest and *Cosmopolitan*'s financial columnist. (Your name should be on the lease so if you break up, you don't get kicked out.) Von Tobel suggests budgeting how much you'll each be able to pay in rent and bills. There's no rule that says you have to split it 50/50—if one of you makes more and is okay with paying more, so be it. What matters is making a plan you're both happy with—and sometimes tossing the bills aside and making out.

4 Do we want moving in to lead to marriage?

Forget your mom's old saying about the cow and the milk. Moving in doesn't mean he'll never put a ring on it. In fact, two-thirds of new marriages are between people who lived with their partner beforehand, according to recent data from the Council on Contemporary Families. Sharing your space can make cohabitation feel like a "trial marriage" for a lot of couples, says Arielle Kuperberg, PhD, an associate professor of sociology at the University of North Carolina at Greensboro. But don't assume that moving in is going to lead to a big fat wedding. Be honest about where you want the relationship to go before you move in, and make sure you see eye to eye on "I do."

COHABITATION FRUSTRATION:
Major Moving-In Issues Solved!

Now that you're playing house, what could possibly go wrong? Oh, nothing much—just blending your social lives, negotiating who rules the Apple TV, and dealing with his "decor sensibility" or lack thereof. We say *pssht*, you got this.

HE: Wants to stay in, make seven-layer dip, and play Halo every Friday night.

YOU: Want to go out for old-fashioneds and gossip with your girl posse.

WHAT TO DO: Go! Having a life outside your new nook will keep things interesting. You can miss your man and feel the sweet satisfaction of seeing his cute face when you get back.

HE: Wants to bring his barf-colored velvet couch when he moves in.

YOU: Are not impressed that its grease stains look like a map of Hawaii.

WHAT TO DO: Convince him to sell the couch on Craigslist, buy a respectable frame for his *Kill Bill* poster, and let it hang in the hallway. Hey, it's his home now too.

HE: Gets aroused by the scent of Spring Meadow Tide detergent pods.

YOU: Believe laundry should be done once a quarter, max. What smelly yoga gear?

WHAT TO DO: Have him permanent press you atop the vibrating washing machine for sex that's anything but delicate cycle. Really, just add sex to any chore.

YOU: Go into anaphylactic shock if you don't watch *Downton* in real time.

SHE: Insists on seeing *Girls* live in the exact time slot.

WHAT TO DO: Buy her an HBO Go subscription for her birthday so she can watch Lena live from her iPad. Think of it as money saved on couples therapy.

5 SEX POSITIONS TO CHRISTEN EVERY ROOM

Do it all over your new place—even if your neighbors hate you.

IN THE SHOWER
The Rubber Fuck-ie

The *surfbort* for people who don't have giant tubs. He squats, you reverse-straddle him. Control the bounce—and treat yourself with the detachable showerhead.

ON A MOVING BOX
The Bouncy Boxxx

He lies back on a sturdy box, you get on top, legs on the floor. Push off the ground for bounce. His elevated hips will add at least another inch to his package.

IN THE KITCHEN
The Slow Cooker

Sit on the edge of your shiny new kitchen counter. Pull your knees up, and arch your hips in a low bridge while he stands between your legs for some piping-hot sexing.

ON THE FLOOR
The Virginia Johnson

No bed? Straddle him with your left leg bent over his left hip and right leg between his legs. Lower yourself and get to "researching."

IN THE BEDROOM
The Tawdry Twist

You lie on your back, he kneels in front of you, pulling your legs straight up. He can use his free hand to rub your clit or breasts. Or unpack your silverware. Whatever.

"One day, my parents came by our apartment for a visit. It was the first time I realized my boyfriend had a gross habit of sticking his hands down his pants and cradling his balls, as if they were a convenient resting place. My entire family noticed and talked about it, and when I finally brought it up, he had no idea why it was inappropriate. Needless to say, we broke up." —MICHELLE, 31

"On our first night in moving in together, my now-husband and I celebrated with gin martinis. Later, he was awakened by flickering lights. He turned to see me with a giant spoon of peanut butter in my mouth and an energy bar in one hand, violently flipping the light switch back and forth. I was sleepwalking! When he asked what I was doing, still asleep, I inexplicably told him, 'Don't worry. It's for the group.' I was beyond mortified." —CASEY, 28

CONFESSIONS OF THE COHABITANTS

Didn't you read the fine print on your lease? It said: Sometimes living together is awkward, embarrassing, and hilarious. These people learned the hard way.

"After I cooked dinner for my boyfriend—topless, because that's what you do when you live together—he decided to Skype with his cousin. I had no idea he had logged on and walked by the screen with my boobs out." —ASHLEY, 28

Let's Talk About Sex

We were curious. Do men and women agree on the basics of what's okay and what's not okay when it comes to how we relate to one another in public and in private? What do we agree on and what do we perceive totally differently? To find out, we partnered with *Esquire* (and the stat gurus at SurveyMonkey) to ask 2,000 men and women what they think about everything from sex on the first date to the dangers of sexual assault. The good news: For the most part, we interpret the sexuality Rorschach similarly, but in some situations, the male perspective will have you shaking your head...or starting a conversation.

DATING

↓

SHOCKER ALERT

Men are more likely than women are to think a first or second date will lead to sex.

If you make out at the bar during a first or second date and then go home together, does that mean you're having sex?

YES

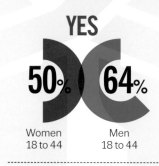

50% / **64**%

Women
18 to 44

Men
18 to 44

If you're over 18, how soon after meeting someone new is it appropriate to have sex?

7%
OF WOMEN SAID DATE ONE, TWO, OR THREE.

18%
OF MEN SAID DATE ONE, TWO, OR THREE.

37% OF WOMEN SAID "OTHER" AND FILLED IN AN ANSWER THAT WAS USUALLY A VARIATION OF "WHENEVER BOTH PARTIES ARE READY." *HOLLER.* ONLY 27% OF MEN SAID THE SAME.

JUST DO IT!

WHO SHOULD MAKE THE FIRST MOVE DURING SEX?

WHO CARES

93% Women   **88**% Men

EVERYONE WANTS HIM TO HOLD THE DOOR

IS IT CHIVALROUS OR SEXIST WHEN A GUY HOLDS THE DOOR OPEN FOR YOU?

97%

OF MEN AND WOMEN SAY CHIVALROUS.

IS IT CONSENSUAL?

When the issue is whether sex is consensual, the difference for men and women seems to be whether or not both parties are drunk.

You're both drunk, you agree to have sex, and one of you regrets it the next day. Did a sexual assault occur?

NO

80% Women   **85**% Men

- -

Only one of you is drunk; you both expressed interest when you were sober. Was that rape?

YES

38% Women   **27**% Men

- -

If interest was only expressed when drunk, those numbers go up to…

Women 18 to 44 **46**%   **38**% Men 18 to 44

BELIEVING THE VICTIM

↓

We all agree that false claims of rape are not common. <u>Two-thirds of both men and women responded that it happens but infrequently.</u> But here's where it gets weird. When we asked:

Should a woman who accuses a man of rape or sexual assault be presumed to be telling the truth?

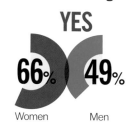

YES

66% Women

49% Men

In turn, fewer men expect to be believed.

If you accused someone of rape, do you think you'd be believed?

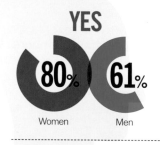

YES

80% Women

61% Men

Many people who have been assaulted don't tell anyone.

43% OF MEN AND 37% OF WOMEN TOLD NO ONE.

HOW TO MAKE A GUY SMILE...

A STRANGER OF THE OPPOSITE SEX YELLS "HEY SEXY!" AT YOU. YOU FEEL...

COMPLIMENTED

12% Women

30% Men

GUYS HAVE LESS SEX?

MOST MEN AND WOMEN HAD ONE SEXUAL PARTNER IN THE LAST YEAR.

32%

OF MEN 18 TO 29 HAD NO SEXUAL PARTNERS. ONLY 19% OF WOMEN 18 TO 29 SAID THAT.

SELFIE SENDING

↓

You like sending them; they like getting them…and then word to the wise, they like forwarding them.

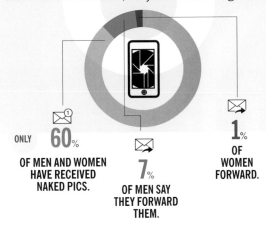

ONLY **60**% OF MEN AND WOMEN HAVE RECEIVED NAKED PICS.

7% OF MEN SAY THEY FORWARD THEM.

1% OF WOMEN FORWARD.

Have you sent a naked selfie?

YES

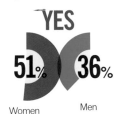

51% Women

36% Men

Also, when asked, who did you send that naked selfie to?

Partner	Crush	Other
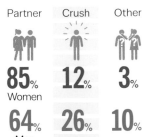		
85% Women	**12**%	**3**%
64% Men	**26**%	**10**%

NEARLY ONE-THIRD OF DUDES SAY THEY ARE FEMINISTS!

ARE YOU A FEMINIST?

YES

51% Women

29% Men

SEX STUFF

Nobody Talks About...
But We're Going There

In your dreams, sex is with RyGos and it's magic every time. But #SexTalkRealness: Sometimes it hurts or he's so boring in bed that you forget he's in the room, let alone inside you. These ills call for a little Sex Rx—and the doctor is in! Now go have two orgasms and call us in the morning.

THE ISSUE

HE'S GOT A
HUGE
PENIS

Emily*, 35, was about to get busy with a new guy when he asked for a Magnum. She laughed it off as bravado…until he unleashed the dragon. "Maybe 10 inches," she estimates. "By far, the biggest I'd seen." His penis hardly fit inside her, making sex painful for Emily and uncomfortable for him.

THE TREATMENT
If he's too thick (think bratwurst), get on top to control the speed and lean forward to limit depth. Also: lube. If he's too long (translation: anaconda), have him wrap his hand around the base of his penis before entering you, which allows only part of him in. Avoid doggie-style (which leads to deep penetration).

*NAMES HAVE BEEN CHANGED TO PROTECT THE NAUGHTY PATIENTS' PRIVACY.

actual size

THE ISSUE

HE'S GOT
A tiny PENIS

There are foot-longs and then there are cocktail wieners. Each comes with challenges, but Sara, 28, is hooking up with a guy who has "the smallest penis I have yet to encounter," she says. "There's just no feeling him, really."

THE TREATMENT
A baby gherkin in his pants is no small problem, but engine size doesn't matter if you know how to drive. Have him try thrusting in a circular motion with his hips—the circling creates a fuller feeling than the classic in and out.

151

HE'S A JACK-HAMMERER

Karen, 23, has a high-speed, high-intensity humper who treats her vagina like he's breaking ground on a new construction site. "Sometimes, I grit my teeth and let him because I know he likes it," she says. But rapid-fire woodpecker sex gets old fast.

THE TREATMENT

Slow down power-tool pumping by getting on top, slowly circling your hips and showing him how it's done. Offer Mr. Hammer a few pointers. Try "I love it when you give it to me slowly." If the pounding happens only toward the end of sex, he might need extra stimulation. For men to orgasm, it requires a combination of friction and pressure on the penis. Try quickly stroking or sucking the tip of his Black and Decker for his grand finale.

whoops!

THE ISSUE

HE FINISHES TOO *FAST*

Kelsie, 28, digs her new guy so hard, "I want him to put babies in me!" she jokes. She's not the only one with premature, er, feelings. He ejaculates so quickly that their sex sesh barely lasts through a Geico ad.

THE TREATMENT

When you fall in lust fast, things can happen fast—think Leonardo DiCaprio's one-pump hump in *The Wolf of Wall Street*. To take the pressure off, engage in a heavy dose of foreplay. It slows things down for him, but fast-tracks you to orgasm before sex. Break out a bullet vibe on your clitoris when you're fooling around, or have your quick hitter go down on you prior to doing the deed. Being able to pleasure you through oral will calm his nerves about the main event.

THE ISSUE
SEX IS A SNOOZE

He's thrusting away while you lie there trying to remember if you set the DVR for *Watch What Happens Live*. "It feels like he's just going through the motions," Kylie, 27, says of the lack of spark with her guy. Sure, Andy Cohen's entertaining, but better than sex? Don't go to that sad place.

THE TREATMENT
Routines can be a sex buzzkill, so think outside the bed. You can't rely on missionary (again) when you're doing it in the car or the bathroom at your b-day party. Send him a dropped pin, and meet for a quickie at that spot. If you usually do it at night, a pre-date romp will make for a very happy meal. And don't forget some "You kiss your mother with that mouth?" dirty talk. It's hard to feel *meh* when you're telling him how turned on you are.

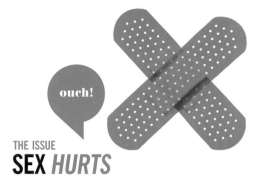

ouch!

THE ISSUE
SEX *HURTS*

Good sex should make you feel like you're on fire—but not literally. Clare, 28, experiences burning pain during sex with most of her partners. "It feels like I'm tearing" when a guy enters her, she laments. #Ouch.

THE TREATMENT
Anxiety, hormone imbalances, and infections like UTIs can all cause painful sex. Often, though, a lack of lubrication is to blame because you're either not aroused enough or you're taking a prescription med that carries that side effect (some antidepressants and hormonal birth-control pills can do this). A water-based lube may reduce friction and tearing and ease the ouch. If not, and especially if you have bleeding (which could signal a cervical polyp) or a discharge or sores (either of which might signal an infection), it's time to get thee to a gynecologist.

SOURCES: SEX THERAPIST MADELEINE CASTELLANOS, MD, ASSISTANT PROFESSOR OF PSYCHIATRY AT ALBERT EINSTEIN COLLEGE OF MEDICINE; SEX THERAPIST IAN KERNER, PHD, AUTHOR OF *SHE COMES FIRST*

Do You Need A SEXORCISM?

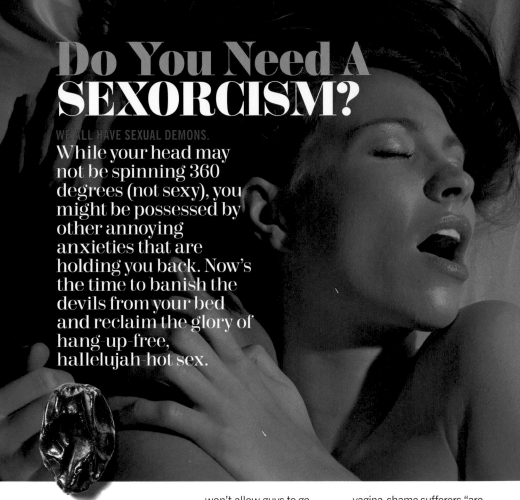

WE ALL HAVE SEXUAL DEMONS. While your head may not be spinning 360 degrees (not sexy), you might be possessed by other annoying anxieties that are holding you back. Now's the time to banish the devils from your bed and reclaim the glory of hang-up-free, hallelujah-hot sex.

THE DEMON
VAGINA SHAME

Getting oral from a man who knows what he's doing is like eating salted-caramel gelato while watching a unicorn jump over a sparkling rainbow. But sadly some women are too ashamed of their lady parts to enjoy it. Kate, 24, won't allow guys to go down on her after an ex told her, midcunnilingus, that her right labia majora was longer than the left. Now, "I think I look weird, so I won't let guys do it."

THE SEXORCISM

In porn, the bald clamshell is all the rage. But there are no perfect vulvas—labia come in a plethora of colors and sizes. Still, many vagina-shame sufferers "are disconnected from their own vaginas," says clinical sexologist Kat Van Kirk, PhD. She suggests a "sexam." Grab a mirror and bond with your lotus flower. Touch yourself using different sensations—fingers, vibes, feathers! "You're built for pleasure. The more you experience it, the more you can share it with a partner."

THE DEMON
FROZEN VOCAL CORDS

He's grabbing your boobs like stress balls and grinding on your thigh like a Maltipoo in heat. At this point, you'd love to nudge him in the direction of your clitoris, but your vocal cords are paralyzed. "I'm scared to ask him to do something because I'm afraid he'll think it's weird," says Audra, 22, of her sexual silence.

THE SEXORCISM
Talking about sex when you're about to do the dirty puts too much pressure on everybody. Next time you're having a convo in the car or on the couch, let him know a couple of things he does that you like before suggesting you'd love more [boob action/oral/what have you]. Most guys welcome a little sexy direction.

THE DEMON
VIBRATOR DEPENDENCY

You love your vibrator. His motor's so powerful, it could rev up a Tesla, and he always gets you off! But things take a turn if you're more into Buzz than sex with a real, live person. "It takes three minutes with my vibe, but I've only achieved an O once from the guys I've slept with," says Kristen, 23.

THE SEXORCISM
Reminder: Your magic wand can't yank off your underwear and flip you into doggie like a human lovah can. So "try making yourself come without the vibrator," suggests Helen Fisher, PhD, author of *Why We Love*. Kick it old-school with your hands and fingers to find out what motions turn you on, then show him how to do the same to you. Try a vibrating penis ring during sex with a human man, so you're both in on toy time. "A man wants to see you come," says Fisher. "Include him!"

THE DEMON
O-FACE ANXIETY

Tragic but true: At the moment of utmost ecstasy, some women worry that they look like a gnarling hyena…or a mouth-agape Taylor Swift at an awards show. Lauren, 22, a lip biter when she orgasms, says, "One guy told me it looked like I was faking and being overly dramatic. Now I'm so in my head about it."

THE SEXORCISM
There's an actual scientific term for freaking about your O-face, and it's not "Girl, you cray." "Spectatoring is when you're judging your own pleasure without fully experiencing it," says Van Kirk. Don't let your face block your vagina's happiness. Try looking into your partner's eyes (or kissing on his earlobe and neck) to focus more on connecting with him and less on what you look like. Side note to guys: Never throw shade at an O-face. Just be happy it's happening.

The BEST SEX I Ever Had

WE ASKED Cosmo readers to reveal your sweatiest, naughtiest, most orgasmic moments and sex tips. You really delivered. Celebrities and rock stars? Check. Forbidden professors and kinky bosses? Oh, you went there. Use these confessions as sin-spiration for your sexual Pinterest board. Warning: These tales are utterly NSFW!

WOW POSITION
"Reverse-Cowgirl. I love getting a view of her butt in action." —GUY, 35

CELEBRISEX

"I was the front-desk girl at a fancy gym when a cute 40something guy who looked kind of familiar asked me out for margaritas. I realized when I got home that night that he was a pretty famous celebrity who had just divorced his wife…but I pretended I didn't know who he was. After drinks, we went back to his place and he went down on me—no joke—for two hours. It was amazing. I didn't have any of that normal anxiety of 'I'm taking too long, he's getting impatient,' because you could tell he was really into it, not just going through the motions like other guys I'd been with. When I finished, he had a huge boner just from getting me off (!!!) but didn't ask me to return the favor. He just took out his iPhone and started showing me pictures of his kids, which was kind of weird. But I still had an amazing time."—GIRL, 27

THREE'S COMPANY

"It was a threesome. I was bouncing back and forth between managing a party downstairs and two beautiful girls going at each other on my bed. I would dive in for a bit before I had to run back downstairs. It was a fantasy come true. Is it possible to peak too young?"—GUY, 27

WOW POSITION
"Good ol' missionary— I'm a super-bossy bitch in real life, so it's nice to have someone else take charge in bed."—GIRL, 24

HOTTEST WORDS YOU'VE HEARD
"Holy sh*t, where'd you learn to do that?"—GIRL, 20

HOTTEST WORDS YOU'VE HEARD
"Your body is the most beautiful thing I've ever seen."
—GIRL, 21

Oral, Up Close

"I made a video of my boyfriend going down on me and focused the camera really (ahem) tightly, so you could see his every motion. Then I handed the iPhone to him to film my orgasm as it happened. I think we've been watching too much *Masters of Sex*. Making the vid was hotter than watching it. We're hooked." —GIRL, 25

BJs

*Cosmogasm! "I learned from Cosmo to do quick short strokes, followed by a slow one where you take him as deep into your mouth as you can go. My boyfriend gasps every single time I do this."
—GIRL, 25

"Make eye contact throughout—and use a lot of spit. The lubrication will make your hand action even more pleasurable." —GUY, 31

"Put a little pressure on the area right below his balls—he will melt." —GUY, 24

"I breathe a little warm air on him mid-beej—he loves that combined with my hands and tongue." —GIRL, 22

Oral on Her

"When he twists my thong around his finger right before he takes it off and goes down there, it makes me crazy." —GIRL, 21

"I love when he teases me first by licking my inner thighs, getting closer until it's torture, then just going in deep with his tongue." —GIRL, 32

"When he props my legs up on something—like a nightstand or his shoulders—while he goes down on me, it's like he's really working for the best angle to pleasure me."
—GIRL, 27

*Cosmogasm! "During a weekend trip to the beach, my boyfriend and I read a Cosmo story on oral. Afterward, he went down on me and, for the first time, used his fingers to touch both my G-spot and my clit. It was the strongest orgasm of my life. We were both so turned on after that, we had the most amazing sex." —GIRL, 22

HALLOWED HALLS

"The best sex I ever had was the night after college graduation with my married lit professor. He was my adviser, with whom I'd always had a mild flirtation, and I had stopped by his office to say thanks before going out to party. In a moment of #YOLO, I definitely made the first move, and he willingly accepted. We stumbled out into the hallway, pushing up against corkboards and bending over water fountains. It wasn't making love. It was rough, hard sex. I asked for things I normally would have felt ashamed to ask for. I did things I normally would have felt nervous about doing. I felt powerful and in control. It was the first time I had sex without my mind getting in the way."
—GIRL, 26

ROCK-STAR ROMP

"My best friend and I scored VIP tickets to see our favorite band—the lead singer is our number one crush. The guy sitting next to us knew the band and got us into the after-party. I flirted with the lead singer while my friend flirted with the drummer. The four of us ended up in bed at my place, having sex side by side, all night. At one point, we looked at each other like holy shit, but in general, we stayed focused on our guys. It was literally rock-star sex! It was amazing. I had multiple orgasms. And the guys made us pancakes in the a.m.!"
—GIRL, 32

HOTTEST WORDS YOU'VE HEARD

"I can't wait to get you home and make you come." —GIRL, 29

WOW POSITION
"I love lying on my stomach, keeping one leg straight and the other bent. The angle is fantastic—and it gives him plenty of fun things to do, like spank me."
—GIRL, 21

HOTTEST WORDS YOU'VE HEARD

"You taste incredible."
—GIRL, 24

HOTTEST WORDS YOU'VE HEARD

"I love the way you f*ck me."
—GUY, 28

Kinky Boss

"I went on a business trip with the CEO of my company. We had some drinks at the hotel bar, and he told me he was into kink. I wasn't sure what he meant, but I was so enamored by this mysterious, powerful man that I ended up going back to his room with him. He had a huge suitcase of sex toys. He wanted me to tie him up and tell him he had behaved badly at the meeting that day. I followed his lead. The affair is still going on, and believe it or not, things have only gotten kinkier!" —GIRL, 30

159

HOW TO HELP A FRIEND IN TROUBLE

When a close pal is going through something really tough, you want to be there for her, but you don't feel sure about how to approach her or what support she needs. We talked to some real BFFs who've been there to pinpoint exactly how you can be Friend of the Year when your bud really needs you.

SHE HAS A SELF-DESTRUCTIVE HABIT

KIRSTEN G.*, 24, MINNEAPOLIS, MN,
AND KIMBERLY MARTINEZ, 22, SAVAGE, MN

KIRSTEN: When I was 14, my doctor diagnosed me with ADHD and gave me a prescription for Adderall. I started taking the Adderall right around the same time I began partying at night with friends. That kicked off a seven-year struggle with Adderall addiction and alcoholism that got much worse when I started college. I flunked out of my freshman year because I was drinking so much, and I had to start over somewhere new. I was drinking and taking pills every day, and no one really wanted to be around me anymore. It was gross.

KIMBERLY: Kirsten and I were roommates for a study-abroad program during our junior year. We had similar personalities and got along really well, but I did notice that she drank a ton and seemed to live on the edge. By the end of the program, I was worried about her—I'd seen her falling over and out of control too many times.

KIRSTEN: I knew I had a problem, but I didn't know what to do about it. Some of my best friends cut me off instead of trying to talk to me, which was painful. And the people I partied with were drinking and using like I was, so I couldn't see how much I needed to change.

KIMBERLY: I wanted to confront Kirsten about her addiction, but I was so scared I'd say the wrong thing. So I tried just to be there for her and talk to her about her goals and dreams and all the stuff she wanted to accomplish.

KIRSTEN: When I was 21, I finally decided I needed to get sober, so I went through a program at the Hazelden treatment center in Plymouth, Minnesota. Kim was so supportive and even wrote me letters while I was in treatment. She never made me feel judged, and now when we go out, she rarely drinks so that I won't feel uncomfortable. Kim just genuinely cares about me, which means so much to me.

*LAST NAME WITHHELD TO PROTECT PRIVACY

HOW YOU CAN HELP

First, the bad news: You can't force a friend to get help, says J. Wesley Boyd, MD, a psychiatrist at Harvard Medical School. Your role is to help her realize that she needs help.

DO CONFRONT HER CALMLY. Stick to the facts and refrain from judgment, Dr. Boyd says—"I think you have a problem" will just stoke her denial, while "You were blackout drunk the last three nights in a row" is harder to refute. Emphasize her well-being to remind her that you're not just throwing shade: "I want to make sure you're going to be okay six months from now, and I wouldn't be able to live with myself if I didn't bring this up." And of course, you should broach the topic when she's sober. "You want to do everything you can to keep emotions down so that your friend will be more likely to hear what you're telling her," he adds.

DON'T BE INVOLVED IN THE COVER-UP. If your friend has a problem with alcohol, you might be tempted to volunteer to be her designated driver, or you may want to just be nice when she asks, "Did I embarrass myself last night?" Don't. "You're enabling the behavior by doing anything that makes it easier for her," Dr. Boyd says.

DO BE READY TO SUGGEST NEXT STEPS. "If you're lucky enough to break through to her and she tells you she needs help, she has a lot of options, depending on her personality," Dr. Boyd says. A Narcotics Anonymous or AA support group could be a good fit. "Their only requirement is a desire to stop," and you'd be welcome to attend with her, he says. She could also contact her primary care doctor or a local treatment center.

SHE GETS A SCARY DIAGNOSIS

RUTHIE LOWERY, 29, AND JEMIKA CRAYTON, 31, BOTH ATLANTA, GA

JEMIKA: In 2010, I was in North Carolina, working on my master's degree, and I developed a swollen, painful stomach—I looked like I was pregnant. I knew something was wrong, but I put off going to the doctor until a friend caught me throwing up and took me to the ER. I was transferred to another hospital, and after reviewing a round of tests, a doctor walked into my room with tears in her eyes and said, "Sweetheart, you have stage-4 ovarian cancer." I didn't feel that scared because, on some level, I felt like I already knew.

RUTHIE: I remember exactly where I was when I got the call—I was in Atlanta, getting my hair done. I was shocked, then numb, then I started to worry like crazy.

JEMIKA: I underwent chemotherapy, and the treatments took a toll on me—I went from a size 16 to an 8 in a couple of months.

RUTHIE: I called Jemika regularly and tried to be there for her over the phone, which sometimes meant talking about her cancer but other times we just talked about normal stuff, like what our friends were up to. I hate to admit it, but I was scared to visit Jemika because I knew she'd look sick and I was afraid that I'd react the wrong way.

JEMIKA: I got frustrated at Ruthie for not visiting me more often—I was lonely, and I thought it was because she was afraid of me! I wish she would've just told me about her fears. Other people reacted the same way, treating me like I was a sick person, and I wanted to tell them, "Hey, I'm still me!" When Ruthie did visit, she was so sweet. She lay with me on the bed, and once she brought me makeup and head scarves after I told her I missed them. Ten months after that first diagnosis, the doctor told me I was cancer-free, and Ruthie was so excited for me. She never stopped being there for me as a friend.

HOW YOU CAN HELP

Your friend needs a cheerleader, not more medical-ese, to help her through, says Jan C. Buckner, MD, chair of medical oncology at the Mayo Clinic in Rochester, Minnesota.

DO ASK HOW YOU CAN HELP. "Some people cope by not talking about it; others want to share emotions," Dr. Buckner says. "Meet her where she is."

DON'T INSIST, "YOU'RE GOING TO BE FINE!" It's important to give your friend real hope. Say, "Whatever happens, I'm here for you. We're going to do everything we can to help you beat this."

DO VOLUNTEER TO HELP. Medical visits take time away from your friend's normal activities.

"Pitch in and say, 'Can I go to the doctor with you? Can I help with the housework? Can I bring over some dinner?'" Dr. Buckner suggests.

DON'T OFFER ADVICE. Unless you're an expert in your friend's diagnosis, leave it to the doctors to explain the best options. "There are many opinions about how to treat cancer, and some are based in fact while others are hype," Dr. Buckner says. Volunteer to research the best cancer-treatment centers, and leave the rest to the pros.

SHE LOSES HER JOB

ASHLEY KING, 34, AND MELISSA TIREY, 30, BOTH NEW YORK CITY

ASHLEY: I worked in online advertising at a start-up, and I was let go in a round of layoffs. As you get older and are paid more, you realize that companies can sometimes hire people right out of college on the cheap to do what you do. It's really scary to have your income shut off right when you finally have a plan and a savings account and are taking care of yourself. And when you work crazy hours with a group of coworkers, they become like your family, and it's tough to see them go too.

MELISSA: Ashley and I have been through this a few times, first when she lost another job in 2008 and then when I quit my job to do something new a few years later. People hear, "Oh, I lost my job," and they give you this face and go, "Ohhh, I'm so sorry!" It's obnoxious. So

this time around, I told her, "I'm super sorry, and I've got your back," and then I let her decide if she wanted to talk about it.

ASHLEY: I don't want the pity face. I want someone to tell me, "Gimme a break. You'll have a new job in no time. Enjoy the break while it lasts. Remember how you always wanted to travel?" Losing your job is kind of like getting dumped—you remember all the great things about the relationship and forget that he was lazy or had the grossest eating habits or whatever. Melissa knows how all-encompassing my job was and all the ridiculous things I had to deal with, so when I'm getting moody, she's like, "Remember all those things you hated? You were on your way out the door anyway!"

MELISSA: It's so important to be positive. When I was unemployed, people would panic for me: "What about this, what about that, what are you going to do?!" That just makes the situation worse. Moving forward is the best thing you can help a friend to do.

HOW YOU CAN HELP

"With a layoff comes the loss of two major things: a daily routine and a big part of one's identity," says Robert Chope, PhD, the founder of the Career and Personal Development Institute in San Francisco. The right support will help your bud get back on her feet.

DON'T START WITH A FLOOD OF ADVICE.

"The person who's been laid off is going through a ton of emotions—frustration, anxiety, and even grief," Chope says. She needs to vent about it before she can think about next steps, and that might take a while. For the first week or two, lend a sympathetic ear.

DO PUT HER IN A POSITIVE FRAME OF MIND.

Once your friend is ready to talk about the future, ask her what skills she gained in her last gig and what connections she can tap into (from friends, family, and even former coworkers) to kick-start her job search. "Once she articulates her strengths and sees the team behind her, she'll feel more hopeful," Chope says.

DON'T ASK HER TO SPEND MONEY.

"Funemployment" means plenty of free time but fewer resources to spend. Your bud will appreciate invitations to fun, cost-free activities, like concerts in the park or pay-what-you-wish nights at a museum.

DO CHALLENGE HER TO THINK BIG. "Get your

friend to talk about her fantasies—around travel, jobs, relationships, whatever," Chope says. "Thinking about what else matters helps remind her that there's more to her than just having a job."

SOMEONE CLOSE TO HER DIES

KATIE SKOCIR, 26, BROOKFIELD, WI, AND NICOLE STAHL, 27, MILWAUKEE, WI

NICOLE: A few days before Christmas in 2010, my family and boyfriend and I were up waiting for my 19-year-old sister, Holly, who was driving home from college. It was storming that night, and when we got a call telling us that she had been in a car accident and later learned she hadn't made it, I just fell to the floor and kept saying, "What do I do? I don't know what to do!"

KATIE: Nicole's boyfriend called me a few hours later to break the news, and my mind just went blank. Her family is like my family, and it just didn't seem real. I asked how Nicole was doing, but I knew there was no good answer to that.

NICOLE: The next day, a lot of people found out via the news, so the e-mails and texts and Facebook messages started pouring in. I really appreciated them, even though I didn't really respond to any. We started going through old photos for the memorial service, and Katie came over to help. A bunch of the pictures were actually really funny, and we spent some time telling stories about Holly.

KATIE: Over the next few weeks, I sometimes sent Nicole funny text messages about little things I knew she'd get a kick out of (like when I found my boyfriend's stash of Barbra Streisand CDs). I wasn't really afraid to joke with her because I figured we should both just be ourselves. I tried my best to keep our normal friendship going.

NICOLE: Some people avoided me—I guess because they didn't know what to say—but I wish they would've just acted normally. I had this weird compulsion to tell everyone I bumped into what had happened so that they'd know I wasn't totally myself, but it created some awkward situations—like, I blurted it out to a former coworker at a bar, and she had no idea what to say.

KATIE: I pulled Nicole into a corner, and we both shed a tear and then shared a laugh and just went on with the evening. If we had to cry at bars, then we'd do it! That was okay with us.

NICOLE: A few weeks after the funeral, my family started a scholarship foundation in Holly's name (HCSLoveLife.org), and friends pitched in to buy bracelets and even plan fundraisers. That meant a lot to my family and gave people something to do to help.

HOW YOU CAN HELP

In a way, grief is like the flu. "At first, it can feel like it'll never go away," says George Bonanno, PhD, a psychologist at Columbia University and author of *The Other Side of Sadness: What the New Science of Bereavement Tells Us About Life After Loss*, "but acute pain usually begins to fade after a few weeks." Here's how to help during those first tear-soaked months.

DON'T FORCE HER TO TALK ABOUT IT. In general, people want to grieve with their families but be normal around their friends—"They want to feel like the world hasn't completely collapsed," Bonanno says. After giving your condolences, chatting about unrelated things isn't disrespectful. It's actually kind.

DO EXPECT HER TO BE KIND OF ABSENT. "Sadness makes someone turn inward," Bonanno says. "People oscillate in and out of grief, so you may notice that while you're with her, she suddenly gets quiet for a few minutes and then comes out of it and is laughing." No need to probe her about what she's thinking. Just carry on as if you didn't even notice.

DON'T FEEL YOU NEED TO BE SOMBER AROUND HER. "People are able to laugh and feel genuine joy while mourning," Bonanno says. Your friend does not want to feel like she's sucked the joy out of everyone else's lives. Don't be afraid to joke or be your normal silly self (while still being respectful, of course).

4

LIVE IT UP!

Design a Space You'll LOVE!

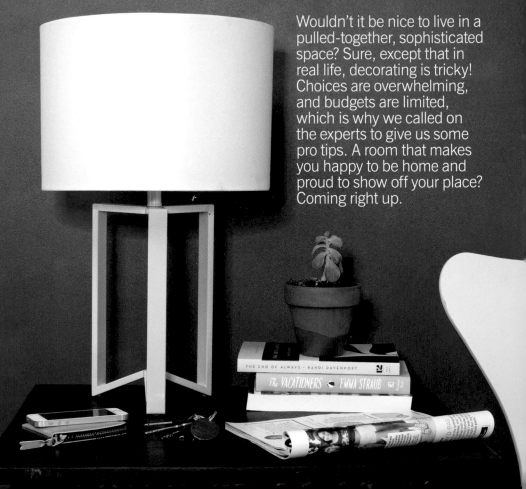

Wouldn't it be nice to live in a pulled-together, sophisticated space? Sure, except that in real life, decorating is tricky! Choices are overwhelming, and budgets are limited, which is why we called on the experts to give us some pro tips. A room that makes you happy to be home and proud to show off your place? Coming right up.

"People panic, and they buy a lot of little things they can acquire easily," says Vern Yip, a designer and host on HGTV. "A bunch of little things makes your space feel like a garage sale." Skip the trendy throw pillow right now, and save up to buy a bigger statement piece.

UPGRADE YOUR SOFA

Target style expert Emily Henderson shares her sofa-buying wisdom.

▸ Is your sofa going to be for binge-watching shows, or are you trying to do something more formal with your seating? That will help determine your style.

▸ Sit on a lot of different sofas. Get all up on them. Don't buy without putting your butt onto the seat.

▸ If you want to be able to nap on your sofa, make sure to get one that's long enough for stretching out.

▸ Keep in mind, a sofa can be a great place to bring in a pop of color. Best part: It's easier to clean than a neutral sofa!

FIRST, CREATE THE RIGHT LAYOUT

Where does it all go? Mapping out a room thoughtfully takes it from *meh* to magical. Drew and Jonathan Scott, stars of HGTV's *Property Brothers*, explain how to do it.

▸ How are you going to use the space?
Will you be watching TV or having people over? Think about the function of the room and how you're going to be living in it.

▸ What kind of furniture does the room need?
Will you be eating in your dining area? If not, you might want a desk or cozy chair to read in.

▸ What's the flow of traffic?
If you have a small living room, put your sofa against the wall so people have space to move around.

▸ How big is it?
Measure your room's width and length, then map out your options. The old-school way is to draw on graph paper, or you can download an app. (**Cosmo** likes MagicPlan or Room Planner, free on iTunes.)

171

Choose Your Paint Like a Pro

ACE HARDWARE HOME expert Julie Richard knows how confusing it can be to pick a paint color—most of the questions she fields are about this topic! Here's how to get started.

1. Give It a Name Think of adjectives that describe the way you want to feel in your room (popular mood words include bright, cozy, soft, dramatic, and peaceful).

2. Neutrals Work In bedrooms and living rooms, where people spend a lot of time, neutral tones tend to be pleasing.

3. Light or Dark? Light colors open up a space, and deep colors make a space feel more intimate.

4. Narrow Down Pick three colors at most, then paint swatches of them on different walls.

5. Watch Paint Dry Look at how the swatches change color with the light throughout the day.

6. It Gets Brighter Color will look way brighter once it's painted on all your walls. As a rule of thumb, it's better to go for a duller shade than you think you want.

7. Get on the Floor Eyeball your paint against your flooring too—it makes a difference!

8. Finish It Off When in doubt, go with an eggshell finish. It is easiest to clean and hides imperfections.

Make Walls Interesting

Make Walls Interesting

"When you're just trying to get from point A to point B with your furniture, color can be your friend," Yip says. "People will notice the vividness of the wall, not the sparseness of the furnishings." Removable wallpaper is an easy way to dress up your walls.

COPY THAT
Pull inspiration from everywhere— literally! *Home Style by City* features rooms from all over the world. *chroniclebooks.com*

GRAB A TRAY
If you have smaller decorative objects that you love but don't want to make your space look cluttered, put them on a tray. "You want to avoid having them dotting your landscape like little pimples," Yip says.

MULTITASK
Go for pieces that have more than one function. You can sit on and stash stuff in this storage ottoman.

Coffee table? Seating? It's both!

ORGANIZE

Does opening your bathroom cabinet result in an avalanche of dental floss and face creams? Nothing will help streamline your get-gorgeous routine like having your gear in order. Here, tips from organizing guru **Laura Cattano**, who tackles three tricky spots.

VANITY

Display makeup and fragrances for easy access.

1. LIP GLASS Recycled candle holders make pretty storage cups. Once a candle is finished, put it in the freezer overnight. The leftover wax will pop right out, and you can wash then reuse the glass.

2. FACE PLACE Edit your stash of makeup and store everyday staples in acrylic drawers. Special-occasion makeup gets its own place.

3. MANI CUBE A sturdy gift box keeps nail lacquers contained.

4. DISH IT OUT Repurpose shot glasses and decorative plates to hold rings and small earrings.

5. SCENT STAGE Show off fragrances on a cake tray. (You can even wrap cuffs and bracelets around the perfume's base.)

THE MESS

NO STRESS!

Your Beauty Crap

THE MESS

MEDICINE CHEST

Kitchen supplies and a little creativity create order behind a closed door.

1. BALM SHELTER How many lip balms have you lost in your lifetime? Stuff them into a short vase or juice glass, and always be kissable.

2. MAKE IT MAGNETIC Remove the shelves of your cabinet, hot-glue a sheet of metal (available at hardware stores) to the back, then use magnetic spice tins to store vitamins and elastics, so you don't take up shelf space.

3. NAIL IT Stash files, nail brushes, and clippers in a tall glass for a fumble-free, last-minute mani.

4. GET A LIFT Acrylic risers create multiple mini shelves. Ditto wooden boxes—just turn them onto their side (see bottom shelf on the right).

5. SMILE SAVER Like nail stuff, dental gear is best kept in a tall glass or tin—upright and away from germ-laden surfaces.

NO STRESS!

THE MESS

Keep sub-sink space fun and bright with graphic wallpaper.

Bulky hair tools and unsexy stuff (tampons, TP) can look cute. Just add color!

1. HIS AND HERS Divvy up your toiletries inside a bright, two-drawer organizer. Prop it on a metal dish rack; levels create more space.

2. ROLL WITH IT Place toilet paper in a woven basket, and slide it under the dish rack.

3. SECRET STASH Lose the cardboard box, and stuff monthly supplies into a cute clutch or cosmetic bag.

4. POT LUCK Planters and vases: perfect for hair brushes and tubes of styling product.

5. TOOLBOX Keep hair dryers and irons untangled by storing them in sturdy magazine files, cords down (and secured with elastics).

6. STICK UP Adhesive utility hooks create a place for headbands and combs.

DON'T STOP THERE!

Bonus tips for the overachiever in you.

MAKE A BACKUP BAG
Everyday makeup goes on the vanity, but special-occasion stuff should get its own bag and drawer below your staples.

PLAY SPIN THE BOTTLE
Put XXL products (hand soap, mouthwash, body butter) on a lazy Susan under the sink.

RACK UP YOUR TOWELS
Roll them up and slide them into the slots of a wine rack to free up space in your linen closet.

COLLECT HAIR TIES
Put them onto a cute key chain and hang it from a medicine cabinet magnet.

DIVIDE AND CONQUER
New use for an over-the-door shoe holder: fill pockets with hair sprays, brushes, styling tools, and more.

STUFF A SICK-DAY KIT
All those random, space-sucking, first-aid supplies? Toss them into a plastic-lined cosmetic bag too.

The Lazy Girl's Guide to Being Clean

Start fresh and clean up your bad habits. Even the most stubborn of them couldn't resist...

• **Rubber Gloves** Wear gloves when you clean. Protect the mani!

• **Mrs. Stewart's Bluing Laundry** renders yellowed whites a bright, bright white by adding a trace amount of blue to your wash.

• **Mrs. Meyer's All-Purpose Cleaner** The wonderful smell is well worth the extra pennies.

BLUEBELL ALL-PURPOSE CLEANER, MRS. MEYER'S CLEAN DAY, MRSMEYERS.COM

• **White Vinegar** When in doubt, grab the white vinegar. It cleans virtually every surface, removes odors from clothing, serves as a fabric softener, and acts as a natural air freshener.

ASK A CLEAN PERSON: Jolie Kerr Knows Best!

Q I recently started living with a guy. How do I deal with the 10,000 tiny boy hairs he sheds all over my house now?

A I would like to introduce you to your new best friend: the handheld vacuum. Dyson's is a powerhouse, but it's an investment. If you're on a budget, try the Best Cordless Hand Vacuum.

Q I put my curling iron on the toilet seat, and now there's melted plastic on my hair tool. How do I get it off?

A Put that curling iron in the freezer! The melted-on plastic will shrink as it hardens, and you'll be able to pop it right off. And stop leaving your hot curling iron on plastic surfaces!

Q A dude "squirted" on my rug. Is there a way to clean that?

A Rolling around on the floor like a teenage hussy! Love it. Semen is a protein-based substance, which should be treated with an enzymatic stain-treatment product like OxiClean. Once you've removed the stain, vacuuming will restore the carpet's nap.

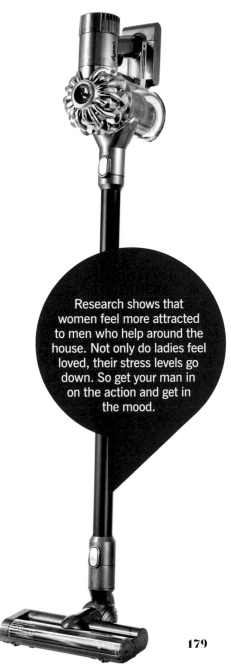

Research shows that women feel more attracted to men who help around the house. Not only do ladies feel loved, their stress levels go down. So get your man in on the action and get in the mood.

179

Control the Clutter

Clutter has a way of attracting more clutter, which makes your place seem messier than it is. So hang up your coat, keep shoes in a bin, and don't let the mail pile up. Small habits go a long way.

DO THE DISHES! Dirty Dishes Left in the Sink = A Dirty-Looking Kitchen.

HIT THE BATHROOM

You never know when someone (parents, love interests, frenemies) will spring a visit on you. When they do, grab a roll of paper towels and a bottle of glass cleaner. Spray the toilet, sink, and mirrors. Wipe 'em down. Glass cleaner will make your surfaces sparkle. You get all the effects of a deep cleaning with minimal effort!

When was the last time you cleaned...?

...YOUR SHOWER

Razors, pumice stones, and loofahs harbor lots of bacteria! Clean razors with white vinegar or bleach; pumice stones with hot, soapy water; loofahs in the microwave.

...YOUR TOILET HANDLE

Toilet seats get a bum rap, but the handle is covered in germs transferred from your postwipe hands. Ew. Go over the handle with bathroom cleaner every time you clean your toilet (and maybe even more often!).

...YOUR BRAS

Your body excretes oil and sheds skin, which creates buildup. Wash that bra, girl! Hand-laundering is optimal, but bras can be machine-washed in a net bag using the gentle cycle. Always air-dry—the dryer will melt them.

Jolie Kerr is the author of *My Boyfriend Barfed in My Handbag...and Other Things You Can't Ask Martha*.

OH, THE PLACES YOU'LL GO

You'd love to sleep in the desert in India, but who has the time—or for that matter, the money? Answer: You do. With a little effort, you can book a #BucketList trip. **Jenny Miller** shares her travel tips.

THROUGHOUT MOST OF MY 20S, I was a busy career girl who didn't travel much. Then I started talking to jet-setting friends and got hit with a serious case of wanderlust. Two years ago, I quit my job to become a travel writer, and since then, I've jumped on at least a hundred domestic and international flights. The lesson? Traveling is easier than I thought it would be. Along the way, I've learned about the world, engaged in a few on-the-road romances, and said yes to experiences I never imagined I'd have, like snacking on tarantulas in Cambodia (crunchy!). You can reap these benefits too. Here's how.

YOU READY?

Research shows that vacations reduce stress and that getting excited for an upcoming trip can make you feel happier.

1.
PICK A DESTINATION

Dedicate a few hours to travel-dreaming. Browse blogs for ideas, and if your heart goes *boom* about a place, add it to the list of possibilities.

2.
CRUNCH THE NUMBERS

You know where you want to go and how long you can get away, but how much will it cost?

FLIGHT:
Look up the price of a plane ticket on a site like Hipmunk, which offers a flexible-dates search feature.

LODGING:
Search TripAdvisor and Airbnb for sample accommodation rates.

MEALS:
Lonely Planet offers restaurant listings with price ranges for main courses.

OTHER STUFF:
Don't forget about souvenirs, cab fares, and museum and concert tickets!

3.
NOW START SAVING

Open a separate online account (like Charles Schwab's high-yield checking account), then commit to saving each month. See "6 Smart Saving Strategies" on the next page for more.

6 SMART SAVING STRATEGIES
SO YOU CAN TRAVEL

Staycation, schmaycation. Whatever trip you've been dreaming of, Cosmo's resident financial guru Alexa von Tobel has the insider tricks to help make it a reality.

1.
Be Watchful.

Got a dream destination? Plug it into AirfareWatchdog.com and you'll receive e-mail alerts when low fares pop up.

2.
Compare Options

The calculator at BeFrugal.com computes the estimated cost (and time investment) of driving versus flying. Using public transit can be a major money saver too. Ask a local (or a friend who's been where you're going) about the best and cheapest ways to get from A to B.

3.
Search Like a Pro

Once the airline spots you searching for flights online, the price may go up and up. Clear your browsing history to get back to the original price.

4.
Win a Vacay

Some hotels and airlines host giveaways on Instagram, Facebook, Twitter, and Pinterest. See what a search turns up.

5.
Now Book It.

Flash-sale sites like Tablet Hotels, Vacationist, and Jetsetter (Gilt Groupe's travel company) secure exclusive rates directly from hotels for up to 70 percent off.

6.
Cover Your Bases

After you've booked, register your purchased tickets with Yapta. If there's a significant drop in the price, you may be eligible for a refund from the airline. Tingo offers the same service for hotels.

WORK YOUR CARD

You know about your card's big travel perks—like free miles and airline-ticket discounts—but you may also be entitled to under-the-radar cost savers, such as a free checked bag, room upgrades at hotels, and even discounts on concert tickets.

CHECK THESE OUT:

▸ **Gold Delta SkyMiles American Express** You get 30,000 miles for spending $1,000 in the first three months. The $95 fee is waived the first year.

▸ **United MileagePlus Explorer** It offers trip-cancellation insurance, lost-luggage reimbursement, priority boarding, and a free checked bag.

▸ **Chase Sapphire Preferred** You receive 40,000 points after you spend $3,000 in three months. You can transfer points to different airlines.

PSST: WHEN IS THE BEST TIME TO BOOK A FLIGHT?
New research says to do it on Sunday. But be flexible about your flight days: Tuesdays, Wednesdays, and Saturdays tend to be the cheapest days to fly. For instance, flying between NYC and Paris on Wednesday instead of Friday can save you nearly $150.

HOW TO GO IT ALONE

It won't be lonely because you'll make new friends on your trip. Here are great strategies for getting out there and meeting people.

GO SOCIAL
Facebook, Party With a Local, and Tinder (yep!) can connect you with other people in the area.

GO OVER FOR DINNER
Sign up with supper-club network EatWith to share a communal meal with a local host in several dozen cities worldwide.

BOOK A GROUP TRIP
Try a surf camp! Volunteer! Hit up LearningVacation.net and GoAbroad.com for programs.

SOCIAL-MEDIA LOVE

As you're posting your awesome getaway photos, keep in mind that clogging up feeds is the fastest way to annoy friends and lose followers. If you're posting a great meal, geotag or mention the restaurant and city where you had it. Instead of just bragging, you want to give friends ideas they can act on later.

DOWNLOAD THESE (FREE!) APPS

▶ Stay: This city-guides app gives you a sense of what you can expect to find in a place.
▶ Kayak: See all the hotels within your set radius. You'll get sameday discounts on some of them.
▶ Hotel Tonight: This app offers same-day bookings for up to 70 percent off. Deals open up at 9 a.m.
▶ Mosey: Like Stay, but user-generated!
▶ Food tripping: Want to eat healthfully while you're on the road? This app will tell you where to go.

SAVE While You're Abroad

AVOID FOREIGN FEES

Buying something in a different currency costs you an average of 3 percent of the purchase price in fees. If you travel overseas often, consider opening a fee-free card. (Just make sure you're not getting burned with an annual fee.)

USE A PRE-PAID CARD

Standard voice and data plans will rack up hundreds of dollars in fees if you use your smartphone while abroad. Instead, buy a pre-paid SIM card at the airport. You'll enjoy a week's worth of unlimited talking and web surfing for around $15.

TIP WISELY

If you're traveling abroad, you may not need to tip as much as you do in the United States...if at all. In many European cities, a service fee is included in restaurant bills. Ask at your hotel about local tipping protocols, then act accordingly.

SCORE PERKS

You won't get what you don't ask for! Ask your hotel concierge, who wants you to have a great stay, if there are room upgrades available. And don't hesitate to make friends with ticket agents, waiters, and other folks you come across, mentioning if you're traveling for a special occasion. Your new travel mantra: It pays to be nice.

How to Travel in a Pack

- **MAKE PLANNING EASIER**

  Use TripIt to share itinerary details with friends and look up confirmation numbers offline.

- **SPLIT THE BILLS**

  Bank of America, Chase, and U.S. Bank have apps that let you pay people instantly. Venmo offers no-fee instant transfers.

- **SKIP HEFTY CELL FEES**

  Group-chat with WhatsApp when connected to Wi-Fi.

187

Road Trip!

It's time to get behind the wheel and go have an adventure! We're all in and here to help you plan the best road trip ever.

Decisions, Decisions...
WHERE DO YOU WANT TO GO?

A road trip is about how you get there, but it's important to know where you'll end up, says Seth Kugel, Frugal Traveler columnist for the *New York Times*. What would you be pumped to do? Explore a cool city? Lie down on the beach? Baseline: Do what you love.

And be spontaneous: the best part about being the master of your destiny is that you can pull over whenever. No one will stop you from staying longer in a town that's better than you ever thought it would be.

Forget Google Maps—use a paper map to plan your route. You'll get a superquick big-picture idea of what's in the region. When you're charting your course, avoid interstate highways—there's nothing on them. You'll find the good stuff along U.S. highways (Route 66, classic example). Hold onto the map. Once you're home, pin cocktail napkins and trinkets from the trip to the map and frame it for a great souvenir.

HOW DO YOU PLAN YOUR BUDGET?

TRANSPORTATION. Calculate gas mileage based on the average cost of gas and the length of your route—then add 50 percent. If you're a good road tripper, you're not going to go straight. You're going to do a little loop here, a stop there.

LODGING. Do a search of the hotels available in your approximate destinations. See how much it would cost to stay at the type of places you're into. Multiply that rate by the number of nights, then give yourself some cushion.

FOOD. Eat "on your own" (supermarket or free hotel breakfast) for two meals, then eat out for one meal.

How to Have a Birthday That Is Everything... MINUS THE DRAMA

BIRTHDAYS ALWAYS START OUT HAPPY. What's not to like about a day that's just about you? Hello, you were born—of course we should be celebrating!

So you're excitedly planning your birthday week, then before you know it, you're cry-yelling because somebody wrote only on your Facebook wall and didn't text you. (Ugh, are any of your friendships even real?!) Birthdays are like the new weddings these days, and while they can be wonderful occasions, they can also steer a girl dangerously close to the 'zilla zone. It doesn't have to be this way. Birthdays should be fun, not stressful. Here's how you can pull off the best day/week/month ever—no diva-ing necessary.

NOW LET'S CELEBRATE

CHOOSE YOUR OWN BIRTHDAY ADVENTURE!

Give yourself some me-time. Why not treat yourself? You could…

> Go on a solo vacation…
> Take a day off from work…
> Skip out early to get to yoga—without having to rush…
> Pamper yourself with a massage or mani/pedi (or all of the above). Take the path of lowest expectations and you might end up with a sweet reward: some QT with yourself.

HAVE A MINI PARTY AT 12:01

Ring in your new year with the BFF or BF… and macarons!

MACARONS, LETTEMACARONS.COM

ASK FOR BIRTHDAY CAKE

But it doesn't have to be cake cake. Pick your favorite sweet and just add candles.

DUFF'S CAKEMIX, DUFFSCAKEMIX.COM

ORDER CUPCAKES FOR THE OFFICE

You'll want at least a dozen—grab a knife to divide them for sharing.

DUFF'S CAKEMIX, DUFFSCAKEMIX.COM

Blow Out Your Candles in Vegas

When you want extravagance, there's no better place. > Start your night at the LINQ, a new open-air district. > Share a toast with your crew on the High Roller, the world's largest observation wheel. > Book a table and split the cost using the PartyPetition app. > Pile in and crash at new boutique hotel The Cromwell. Even birthday girls need beauty sleep.

INVITE YOUR FRIENDS TO BRUNCH

Haylie Duff, star of the Cooking Channel show *Real Girl's Kitchen*, started this low-key (and cost-effective) tradition for her birthday. "People can just sit and hang," she says. "It feels intimate and relaxing." Here's how she hosts birthday brunch.

1.
DO YOUR MENU FAMILY-STYLE
Duff works with the restaurant and sets the menu in advance to make it easy on guests.

2.
HAVE PARTY FAVORS
Tubes of hand cream = big hit.

3.
MAKE SELFIE PLACECARDS
It's good for laughs. Print out pictures posted by your friends, and use the selfies as a way to tell them where they're sitting.

A Few More Birthday Factors

1. Don't expect your friends to pay for you, even if they have $$$.

2. If you're going for epic, you might lose some participants.

3. When you're done celebrating, remember to say thank you.

IMPORTANT: DON'T BE A BIRTHDAY MONSTER

The first rule of birthdays is not to care too much about your birthday. (Easier said than done, we know.) You want to feel special, and that's "totally okay," says etiquette expert Lizzie Post. "But you shouldn't take it so personally." Don't downgrade someone from "friend" to "dead to me" because she forgot. It happens.

Oh, Grow Up!

Or not. The foods on these pages are some of your favorites from when you were a kid…but with a few gourmet ingredients added and some healthier tweaks, they've got just the right amount of maturity—kind of like you.

HOW TO POACH AN EGG

It looks impressive, tastes delicious, and is easy as hell to make. Chris Starkus, chef de cuisine at Urban Farmer in Portland, Oregon, shares the secrets. His advice: Use a farm-fresh egg and you're golden.

1 SET THE STAGE Make your egg bath: Mix a teaspoon of vinegar per cup of water.

2 KEEP IT LOW Set the water (at least 3 inches deep) on medium heat. Let it barely come to a simmer.

3 BABY THE EGG Crack an egg into a ladle to soften the fall. When the water bubbles, drop in your egg.

4 WAIT A HOT MINUTE (OR 2) Cook the egg for 2 minutes. Pluck it out gently with a slotted spoon.

BREAKFAST

IMPRESS that overnight guest with these blueberry pancakes. When you make them for someone special, the morning after is that much more delicious.

Y/N: LUMPY BATTER?
As counterintuitive as this advice seems, keep pancake batter thick and lumpy. Smooth batter = tough pancakes.

BLUEBERRY AND BUCKWHEAT BUTTERMILK PANCAKES

The second these pancakes start melting in your mouth, you'll never go back to the box mix again (and this is just as easy). Thank Marco Canora, chef at NYC's Hearth and author of the cookbook *A Good Food Day*, for this better-for-you recipe.

1 cup whole-wheat flour
½ cup buckwheat flour
½ cup corn flour*
1 teaspoon baking soda
1 teaspoon baking powder
½ teaspoon fine sea salt
2 cups buttermilk
¼ cup whole milk
1 extra-large egg
¼ cup virgin coconut oil
Unsalted butter, for the pan
¾ cup frozen wild blueberries, thawed
Maple syrup, for serving

1. In a large bowl, stir together the flours, baking soda, baking powder, and salt. In a separate bowl, whisk together the buttermilk, whole milk, and egg. Then whisk in the coconut oil. Add the wet ingredients to the dry, and mix until just combined. (The batter will be very thick, so don't worry about small lumps.)
2. Set a large skillet or griddle over high heat, and add a small pat of butter. When the butter melts and goes brown, pour in ⅓ cup of the pancake batter. Sprinkle 1 tablespoon blueberries on top, and press them into the batter. Cook until bubbles form on the surface and the edges harden, 1 to 2 minutes. Flip and cook until the bottom is golden, about 1½ minutes. Transfer the pancake to a plate, and cover it to keep warm.
3. Repeat with the remaining batter, adding more butter to the pan when needed. Serve the pancakes warm with maple syrup.

*NOT THE SAME AS CORNMEAL!

LUNCH

TWO OF YOUR FAVORITE, irresistible school-lunch staples have gotten an upgrade. Check out these mouth-watering new ways to scarf down your PB&J or grilled cheese.

PB&J

▸ **CHOCOLATE-HAZELNUT PANINI**
Spread 2 T chocolate-hazelnut butter and a handful of fresh raspberries on fluffy brioche. Cook in a skillet for 3 minutes per side or until golden brown.

▸ **ALMOND-VEG SANDWICH**
Stir together ¼ cup almond butter, 2 T shredded carrot, 1 T sunflower seeds, 1 T raisins, and 1 t. pure maple syrup. Spread on whole-grain bread.

▸ **PEACH CASHEW-BUTTER MELT**
Toast 2 pieces of whole-wheat bread. Spread with 2 T cashew butter and 2 T fruit- sweetened peach jam, and sprinkle with sliced fresh peach.

3 WAYS TO MAKE GRILLED CHEESE (KIND OF) GOOD FOR YOU

1.

START WITH SOURDOUGH. It won't spike your blood sugar like white bread will, preventing that 3 p.m. crash.

2.

SLICE YOUR OWN CHEESE. Day-Glo American had a time and place—in your lunch box when you were 8. Whole, natural cheeses have conjugated linoleic acid to help build muscle.

3.

SPRAY, DON'T SPREAD. Spritz your pan with olive oil rather than butter. (The bread will still come out crispy.)

GRILLED CHEESE

▸ GOAT CHEESE, TURKEY, AND AVOCADO
Spread 1 to 2 T goat cheese on bread, then top with ¼ sliced avocado and a few slices roasted turkey breast (ask at your deli counter for turkey cooked in-house). Spritz pan with olive oil spray, then grill sandwich over medium heat.

▸ CHEDDAR, PEAR, AND ARUGULA
Layer bread evenly with ½ thinly sliced pear, ½ cup arugula, and 2 thin slices white cheddar cheese. Spritz pan with olive oil spray, add sandwich, and let crisp over medium heat until cheese has melted.

▸ FETA, TOMATO, AND CUCUMBER
Cover bread with 2 slices cucumber, ½ thinly sliced tomato, ½ cup feta cheese, and ½ cup fresh basil. Spritz pan with olive oil spray, grill sandwich until bread begins to brown, then flip. Bonus points: Make it open-faced and add veggies.

▸ MUENSTER, GREENS, AND GARLIC
Sauté 1 to 2 cloves garlic in 1 t. olive oil over medium-low heat until golden. Scoop up garlic and smear over bread, add ½ cup finely chopped spinach, then top with 2 thin slices Muenster cheese. Grill in leftover olive oil.

DINNER

ON A WEEKNIGHT, after a long day, what to make for dinner feels like yet another #CantEvenDeal. Luckily, there's this: a super-easy steak ready in 10 and a drink you pour while it cooks. Yum and done.

FLATIRON STEAK WITH CHIMICHURRI SAUCE

¾ cup chopped fresh parsley leaves
2 tablespoons olive oil
2 tablespoons red wine vinegar
2 tablespoons water
1 clove garlic, finely chopped
½ teaspoon dried oregano
½ teaspoon crushed red pepper
Salt
1 piece (1¼ pounds) flatiron (or blade) steak, well trimmed
Nonstick olive oil cooking spray
2 medium red peppers (4 to 6 ounces each), cut into quarters
1 head romaine lettuce, thinly sliced (4 cups)

1. Prepare outdoor grill for direct grilling over medium heat.
2. Prepare chimichurri sauce: In small bowl, with fork, mix parsley, oil, vinegar, water, garlic, oregano, crushed red pepper, and ¼ teaspoon salt until blended.
3. Meanwhile, sprinkle steak with ¼ teaspoon salt to season both sides; place on hot grill grate and cook for 12 to 14 minutes for medium-rare, turning over once. Let stand for 5 minutes for easier slicing. Spray peppers lightly with nonstick spray and place on grill with steak. Grill for 10 to 12 minutes or until charred and tender, turning over once. Cut steak into 4 pieces; cut peppers into thin slices.
4. Divide romaine among 4 plates. Top with steak, peppers, and sauce. (Serves 4.)

SUN-KISSED
ICED TEA

It's a breeze to make...and to drink.

1 ounce Lejay Crème de Cassis
2 ounces iced tea
1 ounce soda water
½ ounce lime juice
½ ounce simple syrup

Build in a glass with ice. Top with
soda water.

PIZZA

WHEN IT COMES TO THE WEEKEND, why not host a pizza night? People will turn up for a slice, which is why you should follow these must-know tips from Tony Gemignani, author of *The Pizza Bible.*

Mozzarella, gorgonzola, Asiago, prosciutto, sweet fig preserves or fresh figs, balsamic vinegar
TONY GEMIGNANI, AUTHOR OF *THE PIZZA BIBLE*

It's a BYO-Toppings Kind of Night... Here's What You're Handling

1. THE DOUGH You can go wild and make your own or buy the dough from your local pizza place. Another option: frozen dough from Trader Joe's or Whole Foods. Get one dough ball per person (plus a little extra).

2. THE SAUCE Hand-crush canned whole peeled plum tomatoes. Lightly drain. Add salt, pepper, and oregano.

3. THE CHEESE If you want a cheese that melts well and has good color, go with 100 percent whole-milk, low-moisture mozzarella.

4. THE OVEN Make sure your oven can get up to at least 500 degrees.

Vodka sauce, mozzarella, basil
MATTHEW HYLAND, CHEF/OWNER AT EMILY, IN BROOKLYN

Roasted butternut squash, taleggio cheese, bacon
JEFF MAHIN, CHEF/PARTNER OF STELLA BARRA, IN HOLLYWOOD, CA

HOW THE PIZZA GETS MADE

1.
Start by putting 3 to 5 ounces of sauce on your rolled-out dough (on a well-floured surface). Less sauce is more. You don't want a sea of red.

2.
Add the cheese—but not too much.

3.
Now get those sturdy ingredients like sausage and pepperoni on your pizza.

4.
Put the pizza into a preheated oven (heat up to at least 500 degrees).

5.
Bake for 12 minutes, give or take, until the crust is golden brown.

6.
Top with remaining ingredients, cut your pizza, serve, and eat!

Raw crushed tomatoes, pepperoni, pickled chilies, honey

MATTHEW HYLAND, CHEF/OWNER AT EMILY, IN BROOKLYN

Tools and Tricks

PIZZA PEEL
for building the pizza and moving it in and out of the oven.

PIZZA STONE
for cooking the pizza on a superhot surface.

BAKE IT
Sub a rimless cookie sheet for the peel or stone. Find peels and stones at FGPizza.com.

IF YOU WANT ONLY ONE TOPPING
The jarred roasted cherry tomatoes from Brooklyn's D. Coluccio & Sons are unbelievably good.
dcoluccioandsons.com

WASH IT ALL DOWN WITH A NEGRONI
Take one part Campari, one part gin, and one part Cinzano Rosso sweet vermouth. Build the drink in a rocks glass with ice. Garnish with a slice of orange.

Barbecue sauce, smoked Gouda, chicken, red onion, cilantro

INSPIRED BY CALIFORNIA PIZZA KITCHEN

Italian sausage, sautéed broccoli rabe

WINNING COMBO AT A REAL-LIFE PIZZA PARTY

DESERT

EAT MORE ICE CREAM!
Because you deserve it.

MANGO MOSCATO WINE SHAKE

This is as guilty as pleasures get. It's ice cream (your favorite food) and booze (your other favorite food). You've behaved, now it's time to be bad. (Thank the geniuses at Red Robin who created this masterpiece.)

1. Peel one ripe mango, cut into pieces, and put into a blender with the juice of half a lemon and one tablespoon of sugar.

2. Combine two tablespoons mango puree with one shot SKYY Infusions Moscato Grape vodka, 2 ounces Alice White Lexia Moscato wine, and one cup vanilla ice cream in a blender. Blend until smooth.

3. Top with whipped cream and mango puree.

Coolhaus Balsamic Fig and Mascarpone plus Tate's Chocolate Chip Cookie

Coconut ice cream and coffee cookie

ICE CREAM COOKIE SANDWICHES

Math is fun when the equation is ice cream plus cookies. Natasha Case, cofounder of ice-cream-sandwich company Coolhaus and coauthor of the *Coolhaus Ice Cream Book*, shares her favorite combos. Try any one of these and put your sugar high on a rocket ship to ice-cream dreamland.

Mango sorbet and ginger cookie

Mint ice cream and double-chocolate cookie

Strawberry ice cream and snickerdoodle cookie

COOKIES

SOMETIMES, YOU JUST NEED A COOKIE.
Christina Tosi, chef, founder, and owner of Milk Bar, shares her amazing tips for baking the best ones every time.

15 TO 20 SECONDS:
Pop unbaked cookie dough into the microwave for a treat that's perfectly gooey.

DROP-DEAD EASY COOKIE

(makes about a dozen)

- 2 sticks unsalted butter, room temperature
- 1 egg
- 1 t. vanilla extract
- 1 c. granulated sugar
- $^2/_3$ c. light brown sugar
- 1¼ c. all-purpose flour
- ½ t. baking powder
- ½ t. baking soda
- 1 t. kosher salt
- 1¼ c. chocolate chips or candy
- ¾ c. dry mix-ins (graham-cracker crumbs, oats, coffee grounds)
- 2 c. large textural mix-ins (pretzels, dried fruit)

1. Heat oven to 350 degrees. Combine butter, egg, vanilla, and sugars in a large bowl. Stir with a wooden spoon until ingredients are fully incorporated, sugar granules dissolve, and mixture is light and fluffy, about 1 to 2 minutes.
2. Add flour, baking powder, baking soda, and salt. Mix until dough just comes together, no longer than 1 minute.
3. Stir in chocolate chips or candy, dry mix-ins, and large textural mix-ins. Stir until all are incorporated.
4. Scoop or drop the dough into golf-ball-size rounds about 3 inches apart on a greased or lined baking tray, and bake for 10 to 12 minutes, until golden brown.

No Shame in That Tube Game

Christina's favorites are Nestlé Toll House and Pillsbury. Fold pieces of cookie dough into ice cream—she likes Häagen-Dazs Caramel Cone.

How to Drink Like You Know What You're Doing

Whether it's wine or spirits, it can all be a little confusing. Here's your cheat sheet…Study hard at home, then go out like a pro. Cosmo will keep your secret.

WINE

THE WINE LEARNING CURVE

First, learn what's what about all the varieties…

SPARKLING

American Sparkling Wine It won't be as fine as champagne, but you won't have to throw down as much to drink it.

Rosé Refreshing and relaxed. Don't think too much about it.

Champagne Regal, serious, and expensive (also delicious).

WHITE

Pinot Grigio Meet the vodka of wines. It doesn't smell or taste like much.

Sauvignon Blanc Want refreshing, quirky, and a little wild? Here you go.

Chardonnay Powerful and intense, this can vary between oak-y and mineral.

Riesling It's all about honeysuckle floral in both sweet and dry Rieslings.

RED

Pinot Noir Perfumed and elegant, with a fruity and even rose-petal quality.

Cabernet Sauvignon Powerful and polished, with lots of body.

Merlot Lush, velvety, and rich, with dark fruit and chocolate notes.

Zinfandel Easygoing and uncomplicated. It's jammy and yummy.

WHY...
CAN WINE BE SO
CONFUSING?
The U.S. categorizes
by grape; the rest of the
world categorizes by region.
(Chianti is the region that
produces wine made
with Sangiovese
grapes.)

205

SOMEBODY CALL WINE-1-1!

Handle a crisis like sommelier and winemaker **André Hueston Mack**.

Need to impress a client, your boyfriend's parents, or the big group of people you're suddenly in charge of choosing wine for? Pinot noir or chardonnay are safe bets.

Q I don't have a corkscrew. How do I get to my wine?
Put the base of the bottle in the heel of a leather-soled shoe, then hit the bottom of the shoe against a tree (or wall or banister). The force won't break the bottle, but it will pop the cork enough so that you can grab it. If that seems too dicey for you, take something pointy like a screwdriver and use it to push the cork into the bottle.

Q The cork broke! What do I do? Push that shit in! If a cork floating in your wine grosses you out, strain the wine into a pitcher or decanter. It's not the end of the world.

Q How long does wine keep once you open it?
As a general rule, wine is good for two to three days once opened. (After five days, just toss it!) You can tell it's gone bad because it loses pop and zing, Mack says. To maximize the life span, recork the bottle and put it in the fridge. When you're ready for more, bring the wine back to the preferred temperature (even whites lose flavor when too cold).

What does DRY mean?

When people say that a wine is dry, they're saying that it's tannic. Tannins are a natural compound in wine that sucks the moisture out of your mouth. (Think strong black tea—that's tannic too.) In terms of taste, though, a dry wine just means that it's not sweet.

SOURCE: ANDRÉ HUESTON MACK, SOMMELIER AND WINEMAKER

When the waiter/sommelier/wine clerk arrives…

▶ To find a wine you'll like, start with what you enjoy already. Say, "These are some other wines I've liked. What would you recommend that's similar?" Don't try to describe flavors or characteristics ("I like an unoaked white wine") because that might put them on the wrong path. If you're feeling adventurous, ask what the wine expert has been excited to drink lately.

▶ Broke? Don't sweat it. Your sommelier is not judging you, so just tell her how much you want to spend. When she suggests something and you don't know how much it is, say, "Could you show it to me on the list?" or "Great! How much does it cost?" She expects you to ask.

▶ Once you've ordered and the server comes back with the bottle, look at the label, and confirm that it's the wine you ordered. If so, say, "All good!"

▶ The server pours you a little tasting. Swirl the liquid around in the glass (this makes the wine smell more intense). You don't have to be aggressive—one or two swirls is fine.

▶ Smell the wine (it helps you taste the wine better), then take a sip.

▶ Did it taste good? If the wine is to your liking, say, "Great," and let the server pour you a full serving. If something's off, let him know.

Know What to Toast With

FOR PIZZA NIGHT, GO WITH…
BARBERA

This Italian red is fruity and dark, and it pairs well with tomatoes and cheese. Yum.

FOR A PARTY, GO WITH…
PINOT NOIR

This light red is so versatile that most white-wine drinkers will enjoy it.

FOR A GIRLS' GET-TOGETHER, GO WITH…
SPARKLING

"Sparkling tends to be festive, and people should drink it without having anything to celebrate," Mack says. "You're alive—that's reason enough!"

SPIRITS

Drink It How You Like It

You don't have to order a shaken martini just because James Bond does. If you like your martini on the rocks, you can totally get it on the rocks. It's about what you're into. Here's more on how to order liquor so you'll enjoy it.

PRE-GAMING: SKIP IT?

You may think you're saving on cash and calories, but a study in *alcoholism: clinical and experimental research* shows that by sipping before you step out, you're likely to drink almost double what you would if you had arrived sober. If you must pre-party, keep your wits about you by reaching for a light beer or wine spritzer, and fuel up on a carb-y snack like dried fruit.

DO YOU LIKE YOUR DRINKS SHAKEN or STIRRED, SWEET or SOUR, UP or ON THE ROCKS, BOOZY or LESS BOOZY, LIGHT or DARK?

SHAKEN drinks are made in cocktail shakers with ice. They are fresher, often more citrusy, and lighter in alcohol.

STIRRED drinks are chilled in a mixing glass and stirred with a spoon. They are usually clear and stronger.

SWEET Think of a piña colada.

SOUR Think of a mojito (puckery limes).

UP means the drink is chilled, strained, and served without ice.

ON THE ROCKS means it's served over ice.

BOOZY drinks are for sipping slowly.

LIGHT spirits—gin, rum (silver), tequila (blanco), vodka—are clean and fresh.

DARK spirits—tequila (reposado, añejo), rum (Jamaican), whiskey—are full and rich.

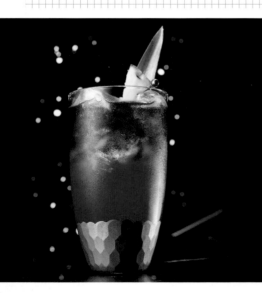

Get Your Glass in Gear!

ROCKS
*Also known as an old-fashioned

COUPE
Not just for champagne!

MARTINI
Also known as a cocktail

HIGHBALL
Also known as a collins

*IF YOU'RE GOING TO BUY ONE SET OF GLASSES FOR YOUR HOME BAR, THIS IS IT.

If You Like a...	If You Like a...	If You Like a...	If You Like an...	If You Like a...
Vodka Soda	Margarita	Gin and Tonic	Old-Fashioned	Mojito
Then Try a...	**Then Try a...**	**Then Try a...**	**Then Try a...**	**Then Try a...**
Moscow Mule	**Sidecar**	**Tom Collins**	**Blood and Sand**	**Daiquiri**
(vodka, ginger beer, lime)	(cognac, orange liqueur, lemon juice)	(gin, lemon juice, sugar, club soda)	(Scotch, Cherry Heering, orange juice, sweet vermouth)	(rum, fresh lime juice, sugar)

18

The percentage of designated drivers who have a blood-alcohol level so high that it impairs them, reports a University of Florida study.

How It's Done

It's happy hour, the room is packed, and you need to get a bartender's attention. Make eye contact, and smile. Then lean in and place your hands on top of the bar. (The bartender always has an eye on the bar.) Be discreet, and keep your cool. Whatever you do, don't snap your fingers, wave in anybody's face, or yell.

SLOPPY DRUNK = GAME OVER.
SAVOR YOUR DRINKS INSTEAD.

WHO WANTS TO PARTY?!

YOU JUST GOT THE TEXT. IT'S GOING DOWN,
AND YOU'RE COMING THROUGH. YOU'RE
ABOUT TO MAKE MEMORIES. SO SUIT UP
AND LET'S DO THIS.

HOW TO BE

THE LIFE OF THE PARTY

HOW DO YOU GET TO TURNT UP? YOU TURN UP. WHETHER YOU'RE HOSTING OR COASTING, IF YOU WANT A GOOD TIME, COMMIT. ONE HUNDRED PERCENT. PARTY YOUR ASS OFF, AND NARNIA WILL APPEAR.

MAKE THEM FEEL AT HOME

TEMPERATURE
+ SPA VIBE
(75 DEGREES)
LIGHTING
+ DIM
+ SEXY
BATHROOM
+CLEAN
+ STOCKED
+ CANDLELIT

LET IT BE LEGENDARY

INVITE THE RIGHT MIX Guests make a party. You want each attendee to be seriously dope.

MAKE THE EXPERIENCE UNIQUE A good party makes you feel like you were a part of something that's never going to happen again.

CONSIDER EVERY ELEMENT Details matter. Think about the greeting, the bar, where coats go. Little things make a huge impact.

GIVE IT A REASON FOR BEING

A PURPOSE OR CONCEPT MAKES A PARTY SPECIAL.

MAKE AN ENTRANCE >Arrive 20 minutes late. That grace period is priceless. If you get there any earlier, you're not giving the host any margin for error. >If you're the host, make your guests feel at home as soon as they show up. Take coats, make introductions, and offer them drinks.

HAVE, JUST, OCEANS OF BOOZE

BUT NOT EVERYBODY DRINKS, SO MAKE A FEW OF THESE TOO:

SHIRLEY TEMPLE / SERVES 1

Combine 3 ounces ginger ale, 3 ounces lemon-lime soda, and a dash of grenadine (or more to taste) in an ice-filled glass, and stir gently to combine. Garnish with a maraschino cherry and serve.

HOW MUCH LIQUID

TWO DRINKS
PER
PERSON
PER
HOUR
+
MORE JUST
IN CASE

"If it's raining, keep them dry. If it's cold, keep them warm. If they're thirsty, serve them a drink. If they're hungry, give them food. The rest is semantics."

—BRONSON VAN WY

HANDLE ANY AWKWARD SITCH

NO ONE SHOWS UP
ACT LIKE THAT WAS THE POINT. IT WAS MEANT TO BE EXCLUSIVE!

YOU BURNED THE FOOD
N WINDOWS; ORDER PIZZAS.

FRENEMY'S THERE
ORABLE. SAY HI ASAP TO GET THE WAY.

TOO MUCH
ATER, AND ENLIST A ND AS INSTANT

PARTY FOUL IF YOU DROP A TAPA OR SPILL A DRINK ON THE RUG, DO THE RIGHT THING. HELP MOP IT UP, AND OFFER TO GET IT PROFESSIONALLY CLEANED—DEEP CLEANED.

LAY DOWN SOME TUNES

Don't start the music too hard. Ease people into it with a slow vibe, and steadily build to your club-goin'-up rager.

ARE YOU A GHOST? >No? Then please thank your host before you bail. Even a quick thank-you wave works. >If you need to shut this party down, turn off the music, turn up the lights, and you'll find that everyone magically wants to go home. Peace!

FEELS GOOD TO GO HOME

Returning to your old stomping grounds is comfortable—
and maybe a little awkward (that twin bed!).
Here's how to enjoy your hometown grand return.

IF YOU HAVEN'T SEEN EACH OTHER IN A WHILE . . .

You used to know everything about your girls. Now it's #AwkwardSilences. Here are fun ways to get reacquainted.

1. GRAB A CUP of frozen yogurt. It's quick and casual, and you'll have time to catch up without any awkward pauses.

2. CHECK A NEW FLICK. Talk before previews and after the movie ends. Perfect for catching up with an old friend.

3. ESCAPE THE COLD and grab a pumpkin spice latte. A casual sit-down alleviates pressure, and you won't have to stay for more than half an hour.

4. GET THE OLD gang together, and go out for teppanyaki (like at Benihana). The fun, interactive atmosphere and acrobatic chef moves make for good vibes all around.

5. MAKE YOUR WAY to the gym for Spinning class with a semi-friend. Not only will you be too sweaty for deep convos, but people also exercise more when they're with others, which means a better workout for you both.

SHOULD YOU HOOK UP WITH HIM?

The authors of *It's Just a F***ing Date*,
Greg Behrendt and Amiira Ruotola,
help you navigate a potential reunion.

HIGH SCHOOL SWEETHEART
He was your first everything, and you truly believed he'd be your last.

THE ONCE UNATTAINABLE
You spent fourth period making eyes at him. He never knew your name.

THE "FRIEND" YOU WANT MORE FROM
You try to pretend your heart isn't shattering as he dates girl after girl who isn't you.

THE BEST FRIEND IN LOVE WITH YOU
He's the sweetest guy you know, yet kissing him would be like kissing your brother.

THE JERK
He loved you to your face, then he bragged to his boys about how he took your virginity.

yes!
If he's down, then go for it. Have fun, manage your expectations, and understand the risks of hitting up a guy from the past. And if you do one thing, put on your good underwear.

procceed with caution!
If this is still your current best friend who you'd like to keep, take a pass on the action. But if not, bring out your inner philanthropist and throw him a bone.

hell, no!
If a restaurant gave you food poisoning every time you ate there, you'd stop eating there, right? Spare yourself the morning-after regret. You know better.

PHOTO CREDITS